"*Fifteen Feet from the Pope* is an intellectual and entertaining treat. Luanne directs her strong analytical skills, honed while working as a highly respected stock analyst, to deciphering the enigmas of Rome and the Catholic Church. Fifteen Feet from the Pope is simultaneously reverent and humorous. Reading the dispatches made me feel as if I had a first row seat to an extraordinary adventure and also made want to hop on a plane to Italy."

—Lisa Giuffra Diaz, Managing Director, Goldman Sachs

"Reading *Fifteen Feet from the Pope* is like receiving *un bacio di Roma!* A fascinating and yet relaxing read. It reminds me of a long visit with Luanne, which is always a delight. This Roman adventure proved to be so meaningful and enriching to Luanne's life, and I am grateful and thrilled that she is graciously sharing it with wider circles, to enrich us all."

—Susan Conroy, Public Speaker, Television Host and Author, of *Mother Teresa's Lessons of Love & Secrets of Sanctity* and Translator of *The End of the Present World & the Mysteries of the Future Life.*

"What a fantastic read! Luanne Zurlo's Dispatches not only allow you to travel to Rome from your armchair, they also provide superb commentary and insights. Let yourself be transported on a literary tour of Bella Roma and the Vatican. Uplifting, insightful, captivating and delightful."

—Andreas Widmer, Director of Entrepreneurship, Catholic University, Author, *The Pope & The CEO, John Paul II's Leadership Lessons to a Young Swiss Guard*

FIFTEEN FEET
from the POPE

Dispatches from a Sabbatical in Rome

LUANNE D. ZURLO

Archway Publishing books may be ordered through booksellers or by contacting:

Archway Publishing
1663 Liberty Drive
Bloomington, IN 47403
www.archwaypublishing.com
1-(888)-242-5904

Because of the dynamic nature of the Internet, any web addresses or links contained in
this book may have changed since publication and may no longer be valid. The views
expressed in this work are solely those of the author and do not necessarily reflect the
views of the publisher, and the publisher hereby disclaims any responsibility for them.

Any people depicted in stock imagery provided by Thinkstock are models,
and such images are being used for illustrative purposes only.
Certain stock imagery © Thinkstock.

ISBN: 978-1-4808-1128-7 (sc)
ISBN: 978-1-4808-1129-4 (e)

Library of Congress Control Number: 2014916529

Printed in the United States of America.

Archway Publishing rev. date: 10/30/14

CONTENTS

FOREWORD

Before I embarked on a four-month sabbatical to Rome in late September 2013, a few friends asked me to e-mail my impressions of Rome and recount some of my experiences. One friend, Sarah, was even more specific, asking that I write about seemingly mundane, daily things, such as my favorite flavor of gelato, so she could vicariously experience this special moment I had been given.

I had never written publically about myself and have shied away from Facebook or most other social media platforms, except for an infrequent Tweet. But I was fully cognizant of how fortunate I was to spend four months in such an incredible city, so, in gratitude and discomfort, I started writing to a small list of friends and family with no promises as to frequency, length, or quality. The list grew and grew, to some 150 friends and family, and I ultimately wrote seventeen e-mails, which I called dispatches, published here with only minor editing.

Twenty years of intense, travel-heavy work led me to make the decision to step back and take an extended break from what had become an unbearable grind for me. I spent over nine years working as an equity analyst on Wall Street, covering Latin American and US telecommunications companies during the telco-tech boom and bust of the late 1990s and early 2000s. It was extraordinarily interesting and challenging work requiring top-level performance, long hours, and lots of travel. Most of the people I met along the way were smart, inquisitive, hardworking, honest people trying to do the best job they could. Many of them became close friends.

Then 9/11 happened. I was downtown, working on the forty-sixth floor of Goldman Sachs' 1 New York Plaza office a few blocks south of the WTC, when the planes struck. The experience led me to reassess my priorities and gave me the courage to leave Wall Street a few months later.

Touched by the poverty I observed on my many trips throughout Latin America and dumbstruck by how poor the education levels were in the region, I went on to found and lead a nonprofit organization, Worldfund (www.worldfund.org), whose mission is to raise educational quality by providing intensive training for public school teachers and principals. After eleven years of building Worldfund, based in NYC with two subsidiaries in Brazil and Mexico, with lots of travel, I was exhausted.

I decided in early 2013 to step back from the day-to-day management of Worldfund and seek my successor. It was a difficult decision. What gave me great solace was Pope Benedict XVI's abdication announcement on Monday, February 11, 2013, the same day I had planned to tell the Worldfund board about my decision. I figured if the pope could allow himself to step down, I could too!

In early March 2013, the week before the Papal Conclave, which elected Pope Francis, I spent a week in Rome on a tour led by Dr. Timothy O'Donnell, the president of Christendom College, a close friend of our family. While there, it became obvious to me, in a hard-to-describe, interior way, that I needed to spend an extended period of time in Rome. Having studied a year in Bologna, Italy, nearly twenty-five years earlier, Italy was very familiar to me.

Long fascinated by theology, but having never formally studied it, I decided to structure my Rome sojourn around a couple of theology courses I arranged to audit at the Angelicum, a Pontifical University in Rome run by the Dominicans. Registration for the fall semester was held during the last week of September, so that is when I decided to arrive.

This is the origin of my dispatches from Rome.

Luanne D. Zurlo
May 12, 2014

First anniversary of the canonization of the Martyrs of Otranto, including Capitano Francesco Zurlo

DISPATCH 1

Arrival

No problems boarding my JFK–outbound plane, despite three over-weight bags chock-full of books, or getting a taxi driver at Rome's Fiumicino airport to drive me right up to my new front door on a beautiful, pedestrian street in the heart of Trastevere. My address is *via della Scala* 17, a twenty-five-minute walk to both the Vatican and to the Angelicum, located just north of the Roman forum.

I arrived about nine in the morning and sat on one of my suit-cases, watching the morning routine of the neighborhood unfold until ten or so, when I was scheduled to meet the owner of my apartment, Renato. Renato, who speaks perfect English, was very helpful and respon-sive leading up to my arrival and subsequently, through-out my stay. I have nothing but positive things to say about Airbnb, the online platform on which I found my Rome apartment.

The most difficult part of my arrival was hauling my stuff up to my new, fourth-floor apartment, requiring a seventy-three-step climb. My goal is not to huff and puff at the top by the time

Waiting to move in

I leave at the end of January, even carrying a few gallons of water and groceries!

Trastevere is sort of like the Greenwich Village of Rome, old and quaint with winding cobblestone streets and lots of nightlife and restaurants. Thankfully, despite the bustle on the streets below, my small apartment is quiet and flooded with great light and has two small outdoor terraces where one can enjoy wonderful views. My good luck continues, as I easily located an Italian-style coffee maker in the kitchen, which makes fantastic strong coffee, much needed after my overnight flight.

After unpacking, I headed over to the Angelicum, the one Pontifical University that offers most of its classes in English. Registration for the fall semester, starting in early October, ends tomorrow, Friday, September 27, so I figured I should get there today. Registration definitely lives up to the have-to-do-things-in-person Italian meme. Despite not having all the correct papers, or even my passport, which I left back in the apartment, the war-weary registrars let me register and were remarkably nice throughout the hour-long process. Having a letter of recommendation from a priest I know definitely helped.

For just over US$600 I will audit two classes, one on the theology of St. Thomas Aquinas and one on spiritual theology, given by two well-known Dominican professors, Father Wojciech Giertych, the papal household theologian, and Father Paul Murray, a well-known poet and preacher.

Apart from these weekly academic commitments, my plan is to spend my time walking and reading a lot, not get on an airplane, and not to travel much beyond Rome.

I spent my first evening in Rome entertaining guests, friends who were vacationing in Rome and whose last night was this very day I arrived. What a blessing to spend my first night in Rome with three wonderful American women. The bottle of wine I am holding in the photo below was shared by the four of us on my outside deck.

My first night in Rome

Behind Vatican Walls to Discuss Finance and Economics

I woke up early my second day in Rome with a rare opportunity to go behind the Vatican walls to attend a conference titled, "The Debt Crisis, Financial Reform, and the Common Good," held in a beautiful conference center located in the middle of the Vatican gardens. Fondazione Centesimus Annus Pro Pontifice organized the invite-only conference to which I was invited because of my teaching position at Catholic University.

The conference provided a sudden reintroduction into the contrasting mind-sets and styles of Europeans and Americans. I have been working primarily with Latin Americans in recent years, so I have less of a familiarity with the European mind-set, specifically the Italian one. I had lived in various European countries as a child and young adult for some five years, but this was many years ago and did not involve discussions about finance and economics.

Conceptually, major segments of Latin America's population have embraced free market capitalism over the last twenty to thirty years, with a few notable exceptions. Those who honestly look at the data cannot deny that Latin American countries that have pursued more free market–oriented policies have experienced more robust economic growth and poverty reduction than the small handful of Latin American countries that have not.

I was struck by the skepticism toward capitalism and free markets expressed subtly and sometimes not so subtly by the Italian economists and Vatican officials participating in the conference. The roots of this skepticism run deep, some believing that they stem as far back as the Middle Ages, when economic activity was organized around a top-down, more restrictive, paternalistic guild system.

Since Pope Leo XIII's famous Encyclical, *Rerum Novarum* ("Rights and Duties of Capital and Labor")—published in 1891 in response to the contrasting evils of socialism and abhorrent working conditions resulting from the Industrial Revolution—the Catholic Church has spoken consistently and eloquently about the need for capital to be subservient to the well-being of the human person as a opposed to the human person being a slave to capital.

Treating people, including higher-paid white-collar workers, in a utilitarian, expendable way in the single-minded pursuit of profits is a modern manifestation of this mind-set. Each and every pope since Pope Leo XIII has spoken out against the dehumanizing potential of both socialism and a heartless form of capitalism.

In recent years unfettered capitalism has been blamed by many in the church hierarchy to have spawned extreme consumerism. After the collapse of the Soviet Union in 1989, Pope John Paul II presciently warned the formerly communist nations against replacing the cloak of materialistic socialism with that of materialistic consumerism.

On the one hand, for many—who view the American free-market capitalism in positive terms, responsible for having generated economic growth and material well-being for the greatest share of citizens over the past two centuries—it is hard to understand how capitalism can be viewed with such skepticism.

On the other hand, an honest look at how so many are treated in the workplace, including comfortable white-collar places of work, and at how shopping has become such an all-consuming focus for so many can help us understand where some of the skepticism of capitalism comes from.

Those who criticize American-style capitalism might take a more honest look at their own systems, how stubbornly high unemployment rates and lack of economic growth in Italy, France, and Greece, owing to burdensome, anti-free market state control and corruption, has created its own set of inhumane outcomes

One element of American-style capitalism, which I did not hear criticized among the conference participants, including those from the Vatican, is our generosity. Americans are extraordinarily generous, and the Vatican shows no reticence in accepting American, capitalism-generated donations.

One of the conclusions I, and a few others, drew from the conference talks is that debt at all levels—individual, financial institutions and government— was, and continues to be, the cornerstone problem weakening our financial systems and broader economies. The vast accumulation of debt has both ethical and technical roots, neither of which has been adequately addressed. I believe the Catholic Church has a role to play in raising the ethical and moral implications of unsustainable high debt at every level.

My Neighborhood Church, Missing a Caravaggio

The Sunday after my arrival, I made a wonderful discovery: Chiesa Santa Maria della Scala located on the piazza right outside my door. It is a stunningly beautiful, Baroque-to-the-hilt yet warm church run by the Discalced Carmelite nuns, an order founded by

St. Teresa de Avila, one of my favorite saints. The church contains a number of beautiful paintings, many depicting St. Teresa and St. John of the Cross. In a special, closed off chapel in the back of the church, one can venerate the right foot of St. Teresa, preserved in a beautiful reliquary on top of an altar.

Santa Maria della Scala was built in 1600 at the site of a miracle attributed to the Virgin Mary. The mother of a dying child fervently prayed in front of a painting of the Virgin Mary with baby Jesus hung under the stairs, *scala*, of an apartment building, the spot where the church now stands. The child miraculously survived. This very same painting is venerated in a side altar of the church where people come to write prayer petitions on a little pad, located in front of the painting, tossing these petitions onto a pile at the foot of the painting.

The church is now known better for something else: rejecting a Caravaggio painting. It was either the Carmelite head of the former convent connected to the church or the local cardinal who contracted Caravaggio's famous *Death of the Virgin* for one of the church's half dozen chapels. The painting was rejected and found its way to the Louvre because the model Caravaggio used for the Virgin was widely thought to be Caravaggio's prostitute mistress.

I attended 11:30 a.m. Sunday Mass, and when it started, only three of us were in the pews. By the gospel reading, some ten others had joined us, a firsthand experience of the low Mass attendance in Italy that I had heard about. The church offers daily Mass and Adoration once a week, which I am thrilled about. The bells at this church, and other nearby churches, ring every hour and between the top of every hour, a rare sound in the United States today. This means no sleeping in late in Rome.

A Few Other Impressions from My First Days in Rome

The other regular sounds I hear from my apartment are of playing children, as there is a nursery school right next to my apartment building. So, while one normally does not see many small children in Italy, in my neighborhood I do. Oh, and lots of dogs! Like NYC, Rome is a city of dog-lovers. But unlike NYC, it seems most restaurants and other establishments allow dogs inside. And compared to New Yorkers, Romans are less fastidious about cleaning up after their dogs.

Prices seem very expensive to me. The cash FX Euro buy rate is US$1.5. By making purchases on my American Express credit card, which does not charge FX transaction fees, I get a $1.35 rate, so I will try to purchase as much as I can on my credit card. Euro prices are more or less equal to US-dollar prices, but given the weaker dollar, this actually makes Euro prices 35 percent more expensive than US prices. The only exceptions I have noticed thus far are coffee, wine, and olive oil.

For the weather buffs out there, it has been spectacular—warm, sunny, in the high seventies. One of the apartments in my building has an umbrella holder outside the front door with about a dozen umbrellas, so I have expectations of a serious rainy season.

I've discovered a number of fantastic classical music concerts from my online exploration, many of which are free performances at various churches. Live classical music is another activity that I look forward to, starting with two Rachmaninoff concerts next week at the National Music Academy, appropriately named Santa Cecilia.

Ciao di Roma

DISPATCH 2

Fifteen Feet from the Pope

I came within fifteen feet of Pope Francis yesterday! Thankfully, I didn't read the "rules" before heading over to Piazza San Pietro (St. Peter's Square) yesterday morning to attend the pope's Wednesday audience. One is that you are supposed to present a (free) ticket to enter the square, but that message didn't seem to reach the well-muscled security guards who let everyone in, ticket or not. I suspect there must be a special gym near the Vatican with miraculous, muscle-building powers where the St. Peter's Square security guards work out, as all the ones I noticed have perfect, self-pleasing shapes under their form-fitting uniforms and requisite Ray-Bans.

Watching Pope Francis live for the first time was an extraordinary experience. I consider myself pope privileged, as I have had the opportunity to stand very close to Saint John Paul II, to shake Pope Emeritus Benedict's hand, when he was Cardinal Ratzinger, and also to attend Mass celebrated by Pope Benedict in Havana, Cuba. Each of these encounters was unforgettable, and seeing Pope Francis yesterday was no different. The pope rolled into St. Peter's at 9:50 a.m. atop his open Popemobile. It took thirty minutes to ride around the square, kissing babies and waving to the ecstatic crowds.

Some observations. Pope Francis smiled authentically the entire thirty minutes, as one can view up-close the proceedings as they are televised on two huge screens at two corners in the square. Smiling nonstop is not easy. The pope truly seemed to enjoy himself and derive great energy from the outpouring of love. He must have kissed at least seventy-five babies on his loop, and amazingly, only three of them cried. I think this is pretty amazing, as I can only imagine how scary it would be for a baby or toddler to be quickly handed over to a security guy, who then foists the baby up to be kissed by a big man in white. I was impressed by the security guy who does most of the baby duty. He clearly has developed an effective baby-foisting technique, right hand under the bottom, as if balancing a basketball right before the shoot, and left hand on the baby's stomach to balance.

Pope Francis then hopped out of the mobile and energetically scaled the steps leading to the platform from which he spoke. (I have become obsessed with steps because of the seventy-three I have to climb to my apartment.) This pope clearly does not like to keep to script. The style of his commentary on one of St. Paul's letters suggests that he wrote it himself. Yet he still looked up from his notes on a number of occasions to add an even more personal, unscripted touch to his address. It was on these occasions when the audience was most enthralled, bursting into cheers. For me, the most powerful moment of his meditation was when, in extolling the beauty and sacredness of the Catholic Church even in the face of all its problems, Pope Francis said, "Men are sinners. Women are sinners." He then looked up from his paper, toward the cardinals seated at his left and said, "These cardinals are sinners; bishops are sinners; priests are sinners. I am a sinner; you are sinners." The crowd loved it, especially the cardinal part.

It occurred me that Francis is a pope who appeals to the heart, and people are so hungry for their hearts to be touched at this moment. Pope Benedict—considered by some to be the, if not one of the, most brilliant popes that ever lived—was more a pope of the head. Pope Benedict's first encyclical, *Deus Caritas Est* ("God is Love") gives a sense of both Benedict's heart and head, but his communication style was much more cerebral. Head and heart are both equally critical to a well-formed person, but sometimes one needs to be emphasized over the other, at least it seems to me.

It was during the moments in which Pope Francis looked up and out into the audience that he most effectively touched our

9

hearts. My Italian is rudimentary, but I got much more out of Pope Francis's remarks in Italian than I did from the American priest who then summarized the remarks in English. The remarks were summarized one-by-one by priests speaking French, German, Arabic, Polish, Spanish, and a heavily Carioca-accented Portuguese. The summaries were formulaic, with lots of fancy words that create a veil over the raw meaning. The pope's language is simple and penetrating.

A "Perfect" Meal

After leaving St. Peter's Square, I had a fantastic surprise! After being on my feet for many hours in the sun, I was tired and hungry. I crossed Ponte Sant'Angelo (Angel Bridge) into Centro Historico and happened upon Alfredo e Ada (Via dei Banchi Nuovi, 14) the proverbial hole in the wall traditional restaurant with only five tables and no menu. On a trip to Rome thirteen years ago, I had come upon this same restaurant and had one of my most memorable meals there and never could find it again, as I never noted the name and this is not the sort of place that has a card, let alone a website. I had just as memorable a meal yesterday, and all for Euro20—pasta cooked perfectly with a simple *pomodoro* sauce, which was out of this world, *braciole* (though, I must say, my mother's is slightly better) a side dish of a spinach-like vegetable sautéed in garlic and olive oil, and a choice of table wine, red or white. I chose the red and finished off the meal with a fantastic round cookie that the owner insisted I dip in the red wine.

A Bernini Discovery

One of the best things about touring blind—just following one's nose and not reading ahead about what one is about to see—is being totally surprised by something that touches your senses without any forewarning or expectations. This past Monday morning,

I decided to explore my new Trastevere neighborhood by just wandering the streets.

I came upon Chiesa di San Francesco d'Assisi a Ripa, where St. Francis is said to have spent time. Here one can view the rock that he used as his pillow. Yes, rock; he was definitely different than us. Tomorrow, October 4, is the feast day of St. Francis, a major holiday in Italy, as St. Francis is one of Italy's two patron saints in addition to being the namesake of Pope Francis, who will spend the day in Assisi tomorrow.

St. Catherine of Siena is Italy's other patron saint, and like the indefatigable St. Teresa de Avila, St. Catherine was a strong, courageous woman and a doctor of the church. She exhorted Pope Gregory XI, in person, to buckle up and return the papacy from Avignon to Rome in the late fourteenth century. She also pushed for reform of the clergy and administration of the Papal States, all before the age of thirty-three, when she died. I surmise that Pope Francis wouldn't mind a modern-day St. Catherine backing his efforts today.

Back to my discovery. San Francisco d'Assisi is a nondescript church relative to Rome standards. But then, unexpectedly, discretely situated in a side chapel next to the main altar, I came upon one of Bernini's last works, a statue of Beata Ludovica Albertoni. Incredible! I was blown away and knew this must be a major work, but the lighting was poor and the description plate difficult to read so it wasn't until I arrived home and looked it up that I discovered this hidden Bernini, finished in 1674, when Bernini was seventy-one years old. Blessed Ludovica was a noblewoman who became a Third-Order Franciscan at this very church after her husband died when she was in her early thirties. Ludovica is buried under the Bernini-sculpted funeral monument, which captures the moment before she died, reflecting both pain and ecstasy. Bernini's Ecstasy of St. Teresa is much better known, created twenty years earlier. Both are truly remarkable. I was proud to read that Gian Lorenzo Bernini was born in Naples, where the Zurlo clan comes from.

As I write this, I am compelled to continue the what-I-hear-from-my-apartment theme. Every evening starting at 7:40, I hear a live accordionist play a rotation of four songs in Piazza della Scala: "O Sole Mio," "Volare," the Godfather theme song and another "Italian" classic, "Besame Mucho." From what I can tell, most of the American and German tourists eating in Piazza della Scala would lose the Sesame Street game, "Which one of these four does not belong?"

Ciao di Roma

DISPATCH 3

An Unexpected Pope Sighting

Sunday I learned a lesson in letting go, *"che sarà sarà."* After a week of home cooking, I was eager to eat a great meal at a great restaurant. I planned to eat at a friend-recommended restaurant and a famed chocolate-gelato place in a neighborhood I hadn't yet explored on this trip—Piazza del Popolo/Piazza di Spagna—the Upper East Side of Rome, where all the great designer shops are located and where the "beautiful people" hang. I have been given precious new insight into friends based on the location and characteristics of their restaurant recommendations. First on the agenda, Sunday Mass at St. Peter's and then my eagerly anticipated *pranzo* (lunch) and first gelato.

I attended a beautiful Latin Mass, with a boys' choir that sounded angelic. There must have been fifty priests and cardinals officiating and lots of incense. After saying the Our Father, the priest often asks people to extend a greeting of peace to those around them. I had never appreciated this moment in Mass as much as on this Sunday. From the various words expressed for peace, or the accent spoken, it was obvious everyone around me came from a different country—Poland, Spain, the United States, Italy, Mexico, and Germany. It struck me just how unifying the Catholic Mass is. With its very defined structure, we were all able to actively participate without necessarily understanding each word spoken. There seemed to be no national barriers between us during the Mass.

Then a big surprise! I exited the doors of St. Peter's a few minutes before noon to a see an unexpected sea of people in the square, just like during the Wednesday papal audience. The two big screens were set up, and there was a large banner hanging from a high window in the building to the left of the square, where the papal apartment is, the one in which Pope Francis is not living. At noon sharp, Pope Francis stepped up to the window and addressed the crowds, to great cheers. He then began to pray the Angelis, a set of prayers in honor of the Virgin Mary, with the participation of the people in the square.

Next Pope Francis spoke to the crowds in his now-routine less-formal manner for about five to eight minutes, focusing his remarks on faith and how difficult it can be to both have and keep the faith. He prayed, "*Il Senor, credere la noi fede*" (Lord, grow our faith). He then asked the crowd to repeat after him three times, "Lord, grow our faith." After this, Pope Francis asked us to pray for something, which I did not understand, during a moment of silence. The whole square was absolutely silent for about thirty seconds. It was remarkable to be among thousands and thousands of people in total silence. Pope Francis has an extraordinary ability to connect with people.

Another word about Vatican security guards. The inside guys do not belong to the same gym as the outside guys, or perhaps they aren't as diligent with respect to gym duty. But what the inside guards do have is ability to manage crowds and discern who wants to pray from who wants to take pictures. St. Peter's is not a museum; it is an active basilica with many Masses offered, especially on Sunday. So, at defined moments, the guards have to quickly erect or dismantle barriers between different parts of the cathedral, amid hordes of people milling about. And they have to make judgment calls as to whom to let through barriers to attend Mass or Confession or the special prayer chapel and whom to hold back.

Searching for Caravaggio

The unexpected Pope Francis experience was a huge positive *che sarà sarà* moment. What followed was more challenging. I took the metro to Piazza del Popolo and decided first to make a quick pre-lunch visit to Santa Maria del Popolo, home to two major

Caravaggios—"Conversion on the Way to Damascus" and "The Crucifixion of St. Peter." I love Caravaggio and hope to see every Caravaggio in Rome during my stay.

Finding major works of art (or whatever) in Rome can be an art unto itself. The-harder-it-is-to-find-the-more-you-will-appreciate-it is the animating theme behind the signage in Rome. I finally found the chapel where the two Caravaggios are hung, in almost complete darkness, on two less visible sidewalls, not the center wall. I plopped a Euro in the lighting machine and—nothing. The lightening mechanism did not work. Argh! I took a deep, calming breadth and quickly walked out, knowing I could and would come back.

Here's an interesting fact I learned while writing this. Caravaggio painted two St. Paul conversion paintings, the first one being, "The Conversion of St. Paul." It is not entirely clear why the second Santa Maria del Popolo one was commissioned right after the first one, possibly by the same cardinal. From the online versions, I like the second Santa Maria del Popolo one better. It feels more powerful and true to life. Here is a guy who just experienced something miraculous, yet personal, and the horse and companion in front of the horse are depicted as if, ho hum, nothing out of the ordinary going on here. Isn't that often the case in life: something that has a great impact on you leaves those around you relatively untouched?

The Emperor of Fettuccine to the Rescue

I was hungry and tired and ready for a fabulous lunch. Il Due Ladroni, described by my guide book as, "Italian gossip mags always feature a few grainy photos of celebs dining at this classy but unpretentious restaurant" was my goal, so there I headed, all prepared with a sharp, Italian-looking outfit. After a ten-minute walk south of Piazza del Popolo, I arrived, only to find it is closed. *Va bene.* No problem. I had the hunger of a wolf (*ho fame come lupo*), but I decided to take it in stride.

As a fallback option, I decided to go to this same friend's other recommendation in the same neighborhood, Il Gusto, a more modern, multi-restaurant kind of place under beautiful old arches. This friend is obviously a beautiful people person. It is located across the street from *Ara Pacis* (Altar of Peace), an ancient altar built in tribute to Emperor Augustus housed in a (I will say it, ugly) Richard Meier modern museum that looks completely out of place. Il Gusto was packed with young, trendy, very handsome couples and families and was totally booked, with a free table not likely to become available for longer than my hunger would allow.

I continued my search to find another, non-friend-recommended restaurant. I came upon Alfredo III: The Emperor of Fettuccine. Alfredo III is one of those old-time, somewhat high-end, local neighborhood restaurants, which is a magnate for non-cutting edge celebrities agreeable to having their meal permanently commemorated with a photo on the wall, managed by a larger-than-life owner and a crew of waiters who have worked there for years. We have a couple of these on the Upper East Side of New York. Generally speaking, the food is very good but not cheap, in this restaurant genre. The restaurant website photo gallery, including a photo of Gerard Depardieu stuffing his own face with a fist full of fettuccine Alfredo, captures well the essence of Alfredo III.

There was lovely outdoor terrace seating. But this seating was reserved for Italians. Non-Italians were relegated to indoor seating. I actually didn't mind coach class seating, as it was cool inside and I got a table right next to a large window through which I could unobtrusively observe the glamorous, first-class, outdoor-seated Italians. The ratio of Italians to non-Italians was about 4:1, and that made me very pleased.

My first important Roman restaurant thesis is: real Italians frequent restaurants far from tourist spots and therefore, without spectacular views. The corollary being: one generally has to make a location versus quality-authenticity choice in restaurants. Despite the non-Italian celebrity photos, Alfredo III fell in the latter category, and I enjoyed the absolute best *scaloppine di vitello al vino bianco e funghi* (veal) that I have ever eaten. *Buonissimo!*

My First Gelato

Onward and upward to my first gelato of this trip! Venchi—an upscale chocolate/gelato place on Via della Croce 25, between Via del Corso and the Spanish Steps—was my destination since I had a generous Venchi gift card in appreciation for taking care of Queen Ruby, a neurotic miniature Dachshund (are there any other kind?), for a week this past August. While I will admit to having a Dachshund fixation, it does not negate the fact that I have observed only two breeds of dogs residing in Rome: Dachshunds and mutts.

There was a mob of people in front of the counter so I couldn't read the uniquely Italian flavors, and I had to shout out flavors I knew. As a chocolate lover, my verdict was that the Venchi chocolate gelato was fantastic, better than the pistachio and coconut flavors that I also chose. But when it comes to regular chocolate, I have had better. In my opinion, the Swiss and Belgians retain their chocolate-making superiority over the Italians.

Since milk and my digestive system are not on friendly terms, I am being judicious in my gelato indulgences. My first rule: never eat gelato at a place whose pistachio gelato is bright green colored, a sure sign of artificial stuff thrown in. Venchi's pistachio gelato was not green and was delicious, but the chocolate was truly memorable. Definitely worth a return visit. I haven't yet come up with any other gelato rules but will divulge them as they develop.

Ciao di Roma

DISPATCH 4

Various Observations from My Daily Walks

I have yet to walk home the same way twice, even when I have tried to do so. There are just too many tiny, winding streets on which to get lost in Centro Historico, only minutes away from my apartment. Normally I keep my eyes gazed downward so as not to trip on the cobblestone streets. But during one of my walks home last week, I happened to look up right at a placard indicating that it was Giuseppe Verdi's home, not far from the Parliament Building near via del Corso. I searched for information about Verdi's Roman home on the Internet back at my apartment but found absolutely nothing about it, only a non-user friendly website about Verdi and a few festivities celebrating his two hundredth birthday anniversary, which was just celebrated. Italian websites or rather, the lack of commercial establishment websites, is a whole other topic …

I have learned that opera in Rome is not great, especially when the New York Metropolitan is your point of reference. However, I am hopeful to get to La Scala in Milan. I have never experienced anyone booing at a performer at an opera, and I understand this happens on occasion at La Scala. While I do not relish listening to a subpar performance, I think experiencing such an honest audience reaction by a typically staid group of people would be intriguing. From my understanding, the Germans are even more brutal in their immediate feedback. American opera audiences are more willing to politely applaud even a subpar performance, though I can truly say I have never heard a bad performance at the Metropolitan Opera. As a proud New Yorker, I think the Met is the best opera house in the world.

I had another famous person's home sighting yesterday, near the

Spanish Steps. An author I have long been meaning to read, Sigrid Undset, lived in Rome for nearly two years around 1920. She won the Noble Prize in Literature for her trilogy, *Kristin Lavransdatter.* I just learned that she also wrote a biography of Catherine of Siena.

Another memorable *passeggiata* experience. I had the best cannoli that I have ever eaten at a Sicilian pastry shop, Dolce Nonna Vincenza, located only eight minutes by foot from my apartment. I personally would choose a cannoli over a gelato any day under 85 degrees Fahrenheit.

Snippet sightings and observations from the last two weeks

- A robust (perhaps *gorda*) fully habited nun walking down a street in Trastevere eating one of the biggest gelato cones I have ever seen, with a huge smile on her face.

- Two men with arms wrapped around each other's shoulders in a tiny street-cleaning vehicle, laughing together as they whipped around Via Garibaldi, right near my apartment. I am not sure if the shoulder embrace was due to the very tight quarters or just a gesture of sheer joy in cleaning streets.

- A US$40 garlic press. Believe it or not, it has been a challenge to find one here. The first one I came across in a designer kitchen store actually cost $40. I finally found a more modestly priced one at a street vendor, but it doesn't work well, and I am hoping one of my visiting friends/family might take note.

- Roman bus maps must be designed by vindictive, sick people! Absolutely incomprehensible. Blind experiential learning (just do it and make lots of mistakes) is how I am figuring out the bus system. After a slow start with a number of jump-off-quick-and-take-the-next-returning-bus-back-to-where-I-started attempts, I have now figured out four various bus routes that are particularly useful—the H, 65, 271, and 40. I first took the H from the central Termini station, where nearly every bus in Rome starts or ends its route. Asking for the H bus stop, having forgotten how to say H in Italian, was a lesson in humility. Word to the wise, the Spanish "aahchay" doesn't work with Italians. My lingering moral dilemma: Must I get my bus ticket validated when the bus is so crowded one cannot get near the validating machine? I was feeling okay not doing so, until witnessing numerous American tourists go to great lengths moving through crowds to have them validated (i.e., stamped by a machine). An impressive show of honesty. I have yet to see a single Italian validate a ticket on the bus.

• Two camera observations: (1) About half the people snapping photos don't seem to truly take in the subject of their effort, the drill being frame, focus, snap, and then on to the next sight. While I may be sorry, I have a no-camera policy on my sabbatical. I also carry no cell phone, as I am on a four-month hiatus from portable electronic objects. On a few, limited occasions I plan to bring along my iPad to snap a couple of key, meaningful places. I appreciate things more deeply without a camera to distract me. Hopefully the really good stuff will stay in my brain. (2) It is truly remarkable the lengths young women go to when posing for photos. The drill here seems to be yoga-like contortion pose, run to the person snapping (usually boyfriend or husband), inspect photo, delete, and repeat until satisfied. I observe that women of a certain age and men do not pose.

Homemaking Lessons

I just learned an important new Italian word, *ammorbidente*. I finally summoned the nerve to wash my first load of clothes in the washing machine located in my kitchen. Figuring out how to use the machine itself ended up being the easy part. Being a New Yorker, I am used to complicated, front-loading European-style washing machines that take three hours to clean a load of clothes. It was deciphering all the photo-less detergent/cleaning supply bottles stored under my kitchen sink, which was my undoing. Rather proud of myself when the spin cycle ended, I unloaded what turned out to be a load of not-quite-clean-fabric-softened clothes. This was a case where I wished I had done a pre- versus post- dictionary check.

Another kitchen lesson I learned during this first week cooking for myself in Rome involved Puttanesca seasoning. I have little patience for learning what spice is good for what dish, so I tend to stick with garlic and salt, which I think tastes good on practically everything. I came across a rather large bag of Puttanesca seasoning near the checkout counter during one of my first food-shopping expeditions. I bought it, thinking it would spruce things up a bit. Lesson learned: two tablespoons of Puttanesca seasoning in a pot of bean soup is 1.5 tablespoons too much.

Our Lady of Fatima, JPII, and Another Pope Francis Sighting

Saving the most important to the end: I had another Pope Francis sighting. The statue of Our Lady of Fatima, which rarely leaves Portugal, was flown to Rome this past Saturday for about forty-eight hours. As background yesterday, October 13, 2013, was the ninety-sixth anniversary of the six Marian apparitions that occurred near Fatima, Portugal, every thirteenth day of the month from June through October in 1917. Mary appeared to three poor shepherd children, two of whom passed soon after the apparitions, and the third, Lucia, who just passed away in 2005 at the age of ninety-seven.

During the five apparitions leading up to the sixth and final October 13 apparition, Mary told the three children that a miracle would occur on October 13. The morning of October 13, 1917, was beset with torrential rains, but despite this, some seventy thousand people were reported to have shown up to witness the miracle, including a number of news outlets. What they witnessed was the miracle of the sun, in which the sun danced in the sky and was able to be viewed directly by the human eye without blinding the person. Various-colored rays also emanated from the sun during its miraculous movements.

Pope John Paul II was shot in St. Peter's square on May 13, 1981. He came very close to death and attributed his life being saved to Our Lady of Fatima. After JPII recovered, he commissioned a painting of the Virgin Mary be painted on the corner wall of one of the brick buildings to the right of St. Peter's Square. Why? Right after he was shot, he searched for an image of Mary in St. Peter's Square and could not find one. He also made a pilgrimage to Fatima and brought the very bullet that lodged in his chest from the gunshot. This bullet is now embedded in this same Our Lady of Fatima statue that was venerated by Pope Francis and carried in a procession around St. Peter's Square this past Saturday.

Pope Francis led a prayer service and rosary with the statue in St. Peter's Square on Saturday afternoon. It was beautiful. The pope seemed tired, but by the very end of his remarks, he perked up a bit. Pope Francis said a special 10:30 a.m. Mass yesterday (Sunday) in St. Peter's Square, which I watched live from my apartment, and again, I must say he seemed very tired to me. It is hard to imagine carrying his responsibilities at the age of seventy-six. After the Mass, Pope Francis consecrated the world to the Immaculate Heart of Mary. Like Pope JPII and Pope Benedict, Pope Francis has a deep Marian devotion.

Ciao di Roma

DISPATCH 5

A Sad Moment in Rome's Past

Today, October 16, 2013, is the seventieth anniversary of the brutal round-up of Roman Jews by the city's German Nazi occupiers who had seized Rome after Mussolini's Fascist government fell in July 1943. Between ten thousand and eleven thousand Jews lived in Rome in 1943, the vast majority in a ghetto located next to the Tiber River, across from Trastevere, where I live, and where Rome's Jews lived until the early Middle Ages.

Of these ten to eleven thousand Jews, 1,022 (two hundred children) were seized by Nazis in a dawn raid on the morning of October 16, 1943, and sent to Auschwitz. Only sixteen survived, fifteen men and one woman. In all of Italy in 1943, there were an estimated forty-five thousand Jews, with a heavier concentration in the north. Of these forty-five thousand Jews, 6,806 were deported, 5,969 of whom were murdered, and 837 survived. Mid-Italy to the north came under Nazi occupation after Mussolini's fall and the south of Italy and islands came under Allied occupation.

Providentially (I don't believe in coincidences), I spent yesterday afternoon exploring the Jewish neighborhood of Rome, ate at a Jewish-Italian restaurant, and spent a few hours at the Museo Ebraico, connected to Rome's largest synagogue. Today, there are sixteen synagogues in Rome and an estimated twelve to thirteen thousand Jews, some three thousand of whom are relatively recent émigrés or refugees from Libya.

I bought a book at the museum titled, *The Racial Laws and the Jewish Community of Rome 1938–1945,* which is where my figures come from. Reading this book, I learned that some thirty-five pieces of legislation against Italian Jews were approved by the

Ministerial Council of Mussolini's government before the German occupation, starting in September 1938, as Mussolini was developing closer relations with Hitler, leading up to the Iron Pact of 1939. Prior to yesterday, I had been under the impression that Italy's culpability with respect to how Jews were treated before and during WWII was limited to *after* the Nazi occupation.

Two weeks prior to the round-up, the Nazi SS had broken into the offices of the Roman Jewish Community and stole its registers and documents (and money), helping the Nazis identify the names and addresses of Roman Jews. Some 90 percent of Roman Jews found refuge in the homes of non-Jewish citizens, many from some of Rome's oldest and most prominent families, and in Rome's many convents and seminaries, in response to explicit requests by Pope Pius XII.

In Defense of Pope Pius XII

Pope Pius XII has been slandered mercilessly since his death in 1958. What many do not appear to appreciate is the extreme dilemma he faced. Pope Pius had two stark options: speak out assertively against the Nazis and their unspeakable brutality against the Jews, a tactic that had proven disastrous, or speak in more veiled terms and quietly, but aggressively, work to physically save as many Jews as possible. Pius XII chose the second option and is excoriated for it.

Albrecht von Kessel, an official at the German Embassy to the Holy See during the war, and active in the anti-Nazi resistance, wrote in 1963: "We were convinced that a fiery protest by Pius XII against the persecution of the Jews … would certainly not have saved the life of a single Jew. Hitler, like a trapped beast, would react to any menace that he felt directed at him, with cruel violence."

The Catholic clergy of Holland were the most vocal in their protest against Jewish persecutions. As a result, 79 percent of Dutch Jews were deported, more than anywhere else in Western Europe.

A former inmate of Dachau, Msgr. Jean Bernard, later bishop

of Luxembourg, wrote in *Priestblock 25487: A Memoir of Dachau*: "The detained priests trembled every time news reached us of some protest by a religious authority, but particularly by the Vatican. We all had the impression that our warders made us atone heavily for the fury these protests evoked." More than eight thousand Catholic priests in Germany came in open conflict with the Third Reich and were subsequently threatened, beaten, imprisoned, or killed by the regime, representing well over one-third of Germany's priests. I do not think many people know this.

Pius XII supervised a rescue network, which saved an estimated eight hundred thousand–plus Jewish lives, more than all the international agencies put together. It is estimated that 60 to 65 percent of Europe's Jews were exterminated during WWII. "Only" 10 percent of Roman Jews were exterminated due, in large measure, to the efforts of Pope Pius XII.

Of the estimated ten to eleven thousand Jews who lived in Rome on the tragic morning of October 16, 1943, when the Nazis conducted a brutal roundup of the city's Jews, 1,022 were captured, thanks to a warning from the Vatican to Rome's chief rabbi, Israel Zolli, who later converted to Catholicism, taking the Baptism name Eugenio, Pope Pius XII's birth name.

Pope Pius XII had a deep love and appreciation for the Jews, as reflected in first-person accounts by many of the thousands of Roman Jews who found refuge behind Vatican walls, in Roman convents and seminaries, and in the Apostolic Palace of Castel Gandolfo, where smoke marks from cooking fires lit by Jewish refugees during the Nazi occupation remain today.

In appreciation of Pope Pius XII, Jewish refugees hidden in Castel Gandolfo presented him a large handmade cross after the war. Rather than display this cross in a more prominent location, like the Vatican Museum, Pope Pius XII asked that this cross remain in the basement of Castel Gandolfo to commemorate the Jews who suffered there.

After the end of WWII, Pius XII received a large delegation of

Roman Jews to the Vatican, opening up the Imperial steps that are normally reserved for heads of state. He welcomed them warmly saying, "I am only the vicar of Christ, but you are his very kith and kin."

Jewish historian, theologian, and Israeli diplomat Pinchas Lapide sums up Pius XII's role this way, "Unable to cure the sickness of an entire civilization, and unwilling to bear the brunt of Hitler's fury, the Pope, unlike many far mightier than he, alleviated, relieved, retrieved, appealed, petitioned—and saved as best he could by his own lights. Who, but a prophet or a martyr could have done much more?"

Today, in Rome's main synagogue, commemorative services began at 5:30 a.m., the time at which the raid started. For anyone visiting Rome, I highly recommend visiting the Museo Ebraico. I also highly recommend the 1970 movie *Garden of the Finzi-Continis* about a bourgeois Jewish Ferrara family leading up to WWII and their eventual deportation. I saw this movie about fifteen years ago and still remember it in great detail. *The Finzi-Continis*, along with Roberto Benigni's *Life Is Beautiful,* touchingly address the fate of Italian Jews in WWII.

A Roman Jewish Meal

To end this dispatch on a less-somber note, I will make mention of the terrific fried artichokes, *carciofi alla giudia,* I enjoyed for lunch at Ba'Ghetto, Via Portico d'Ottavia 57. More than 50 percent of the men eating there were wearing yarmulkes, and interestingly, most of these men were American. I ended up sitting next to a lovely Jewish American couple from Chicago who had just arrived to Rome yesterday morning. I then realized that this is a destination restaurant for American Jews. As a NYC Upper West Sider, I felt right at home.

The one little dig I will make of the American tourists I have observed in Rome thus far is that most do not attempt to speak even a rudimentary word or phrase in Italian, such as *per favore* or *grazie*. The one thing I really appreciate about the tourist-fatigued Romans is that they really do indulge one's feeble attempts at speaking Italian. I cannot count the times a Roman merchant will start speaking English to me after enduring just a few words of my "Italian." But when I stick to my Italian, they go along with it, patiently. While Italy's neighbors to the west may be overly maligned for their lack of *patience avec les Americans*, they certainly are not as linguistically accommodating as the Italians.

As a nod to my Brazilian friends, in addition to the fried artichokes, I also ordered the typical Roman Jewish dish, salted cod *baccala*, cooked Sicilian style. The *baccala* I have eaten in Brazil has been better than what I had yesterday in Rome.

Ciao di Roma

DISPATCH 6

My Own Roman Holiday

This morning, I rented a Vespa and whizzed around Rome. Without a doubt, this was one of the most harrowing and fun experiences I have had in a very long time! I was rather pleased with myself for conquering my initial fear, so I asked Francesco, the man who rented me the Vespa, to snap the attached photo before setting off.

My Vespa and me

I had happened upon Francesco's bike-Vespa rental shop by accident some two weeks ago while getting lost on the way to my first day of classes. One moment I was walking under a fantastically blue Roman sky, and the next moment I had to run for cover from a sudden torrential rain shower. This is how I found Francesco's bike rental business. While waiting for the rain to stop, he convinced me that renting a Vespa would be fun and *no c'è problema.*

I remained doubtful but couldn't get the idea out of my mind. What finally convinced me to give it a go was seeing sheer fear on the faces of a group of German tourists trying to keep up with their Italian leader on Segways near Piazza Venezia a few days prior. I figured if these folks could ride Segways on the Rome streets for what looked to be the first time, I could try a Vespa.

Despite our respective Italian-English language limitations, Francesco was able to explain to me how it worked. When it became obvious during his explanation that I wasn't an experienced Vespa pilot, or any sort of motorcycle kind of thing, he asked me point blank if I had actually ever ridden one. Figuring my answer could have important consequences I told him *certamente,* remembering that some twenty-five years ago I was a passenger on a Vespa while visiting Florence, with someone else driving. He did use the verb "ride" versus "drive," no? Francesco's confidence in me dissipated rapidly throughout the exchange, but finally he did let me wobble off, yelling from behind, *"Piano, piano!"* The first twenty minutes were sheer terror. But gradually, I got the hang of it and then loved every moment!

Having learned how to drive in Boston, I will defend Roman drivers. Based on my four-hour Vespa experience, I will defend Roman drivers as being better and even more accommodating than Boston drivers! I took Francesco's *"piano, piano"* plea to heart and kept it very slow. Only twice was I beeped at for not going faster, by men in little sports cars.

The reaction my Vespa and I evoked was fascinating. Young men passing by in cars (everyone passed me) generally expressed looks of curiosity bordering on modest disgust, as my *piano* velocity must have represented a betrayal of the two-wheel motor class. Older men, however, seemed totally enamored with my

Vespa. While stopped, either at a red light or during my three little breaks, older guys asked me what model of Vespa I was driving and whether it was automatic. Two men cited stories of past Vespas they owned. There seems to be a great appreciation for the machine.

My friend Diego, expert on all things Roman, informed me that Vespas evoked nostalgia, especially among older generations, since no one rides Vespas anymore. Hearing this, I realized that, indeed, I had seen no other Vespas on the road during my ride! Rome has become a motorcycle city. Why? Motorcycles are faster than Vespas.

Curious, I learned that the first Vespa was produced right after the end of WWII, in 1946, by Piaggio & Co., a former fighter plane manufacturer located near Pisa. Given the grim state of Italy's economy, the desperate need for an affordable mode of transportation, and poor road infrastructure, Enrico Piaggio, the founder's son, shifted the strategic direction of the company away from planes to Vespas. Enrico himself came up with the name. Upon seeing the first prototype, he is reputed to have exclaimed, "*Sembra una vespa!*" Vespa means wasp in Italian (and Latin). In the late 1940s between thirty and fifty thousand Vespas were sold annually. Thanks to *Roman Holiday,* Vespa sales exploded, doubling to one hundred thousand in 1952 alone.

There is no better way to explore the outer reaches of Rome or the hill areas than on a Vespa. My first destination was the Aventine, the hill area above the Roman Forum. Following my nose, and my limited Vespa turning ability, I came to a beautiful little square, Piazza de Cavalieri di Malta, site of the famous Villa Malta keyhole, which provides a fantastic view of the Vatican. I had vaguely remembered hearing about some famous keyhole in Rome. Since there was a line of about ten people waiting to look through this keyhole, I decided it was worth checking out and I made my first stop, right beside the keyhole gathering.

A lesson in humility was quickly had. I was able to turn off the motor without a problem. It was lifting the Vespa up and back to balance it on its kick-stand that proved impossible for me. I am strong, but for the life of me, I could not get the Vespa set upon its kickstand so it would stay upright. Finally, a pitying older Italian man and his wife broke the line and came over offering to help, which I readily accepted. The man then spent the next five minutes admiring my Vespa and told me about his old Vespa. Nostalgia.

St. Cecilia and the 1960 Olympic Village

From the Aventine, I rode along the Tiber toward the north of Rome to check out Rome's new major music venue, Auditorium Parco della Musica, which houses the famous Academia Nazionale di Cecilia, the oldest music institution in the world, founded by papal bull in 1585. Saint Cecilia was a Roman noblewoman who lived in the second century AD and is one of the most-venerated martyrs of Christian antiquity.

Legend has it that St. Cecilia was struck three times with a sword on her neck but didn't die for three days, during which she sang beautifully. St. Cecilia is the patron saint of musicians, poets, and church music, and her feast day is November 22. There is a hauntingly beautiful statue of St. Cecilia, with a neck wound, at the Church of St. Cecilia in my Trastevere neighborhood. I hope to attend a concert at the church on her feast day.

Next to the music auditorium is Rome's 1960 Olympic Village, which was purposefully built to be converted into residential housing after the Olympics. Every street is named after a different country. I loved the look and feel of this neighborhood. I later read that the area came under some disrepair in the 1980s, when an apartment could be purchased for about 20,000 Euros. The neighborhood has been gentrified, partly due to the new world-class music auditorium. Apartments in the Olympic Village now go for half a million Euros.

Luanne D. Zurlo

Riding Home

My four hours were starting to run out, so I headed home from this northern part of Rome, only to discover that when I got back to my Trastevere neighborhood, all the streets are one-way. One doesn't take note of this when walking. Thankfully, the two motorcycle-mounted *Carabinieri* who alerted me to this fact let me turn around with exasperated shrugs.

As I rolled up to Francesco's rental place, I noticed the gates were locked, so I parked the Vespa, having now figured out how to get it up on its kick-stand after a few tries, and climbed the seventy-three steps up to my apartment to Skype him (per my no–cell-phone policy), only to be told that he was in the middle of his pasta course and that I should come back in a few hours. I had assumed that he would have been eagerly awaiting his precious Vespa's return. Clearly, Francesco had other more important priorities at that moment.

DISPATCH 7

Becoming Roman

This past week I made great strides on the path to becoming Roman. Since my Vespa adventure last Saturday, I stopped carrying the ubiquitous tourist badge of honor—"*la pianta*" (map). Rome is not an easy city to navigate. Unlike Renaissance architects, Roman city planners had an aversion to perpendicular angles. It is said that Boston's winding city streets are the remnant of meandering cow paths. I am reading the highly recommended book on Roman history, *Rome: A Cultural, Visual and Personal History*, by Robert Hughes. I still have not come to the part where the origins of Rome's jigsaw puzzle–shaped road layout are explained.

Another becoming-Roman experience: Four different people asked me for directions this week, two of whom were Italian! Of course, I knew how to help the tourists because they want to get to spots I, as a former tourist, had already been to. It was the two Italians I could not help with an apologetic, *non lo so*.

And the most impressive test of being Roman—crossing the major arteries that merge into Piazza de Venezia in front of the white wedding cake Vittorio Emanuele II monument next to the Roman Forum. This is a major road convergence point and one I have to pass three days a week on my way to class. Rules, and how they are enforced in Italy, require a dissertation unto itself, and I am sure many already have been written. From what I observe, the expression "possession is nine-tenths of the law" most succinctly describes how traffic laws are enforced in Rome.

Pedestrians as Moses

As hard as it is to believe, Rome is a pedestrian-friendly city, with hashed crosswalks everywhere. Cars, massive tour buses, motorcycles, and Vespas are all required, by law, to stop for pedestrians in crosswalks. As a little bitty, single pedestrian facing mobs of vehicular traffic speeding by, it is hard to imagine that one has the right of way.

Traffic will not yield to tentative pedestrians, however. Drivers will only yield to courageous pedestrians willing to foist themselves onto oncoming traffic with a purposeful, forward look and an I-own-this-road attitude. Incredibly, it works. Until last week, I couldn't muster this attitude, so I would wait for savvy Italians to begin crossing and discretely follow closely on their heels. I came by some *coraggio* this week, and incredibly, when I stepped out purposefully, not looking right or left, all traffic stopped in both directions! It seriously felt like the opening of the Red Sea for Moses. I now look with empathy upon tourists at crosswalks waiting for the nonexistent green light.

Daily Walk Observations

There is a delicately choreographed dance between Rome's immigrant street vendors and the Italian *Carabinieri*. As in NYC, raw capitalism is at work at the über tourist spots, and like in NYC, the favored products being sold are copy designer bags and watches. Immigrant vendors utilize an array of various display contraptions. The moment a *Carabinieri* comes in sight, the display apparatus and all its goods are folded up in haste before the vendor then saunters off. Looking at the faces of the *Carabinieri*, it is obvious they know what is going on, and within a moment of their departure, the vendors are back in business. The rapidity with which Roman and New York umbrella vendors appear at the first drop of rain is equally impressive.

There is a defined turf system worked out by the all-too-many beggars who have become fixtures on the streets. Now that I am starting to repeat my routes, I notice the same beggars at exactly the same spots each day. When one is in a new place, things hit one more viscerally so. While I see many beggars in NYC, the ones I see here seem to bother me more for some reason.

There is a crippled man who begs on the Ponte Sisto, which I cross practically every day. I gave him one or two Euros on my way to class one morning, and when I came back that afternoon, instead of holding out his hat for another handout, he bowed to thank me, as he remembered my modest gesture that morning. And the following morning, he also bowed to thank me. I am more than happy to extend regular acts of charity to him, but many beggars seem less authentically or truly needy, in some inexplicable way.

Rome According to Father Diego

A Canadian Jesuit I know who was spending a few weeks in Rome studying Italian while I was there introduced me to Father Diego, a Spanish Jesuit. Diego is an expert on Luis de Molina, a sixteenth-century Spanish Jesuit Scholastic who, along with a handful of confreres, developed the concept of the time value of money. This Spanish group of theologians is also credited with making the theological argument for allowing interest to be charged on certain types of debt and for developing the field of economics as a distinct area of study.

Having lived in Rome for a few years already, Diego kindly let me in on all he had already learned about things Roman. One day, while driving back into Centro Historico after a weekend trip with his mother, the roads around his residence were all blocked to traffic for some inexplicable reason. The first *Carabinieri* blocking a road that Diego and his mother stopped at insisted he turn around, as did the second *Carabinieri* at another road leading to his destination. At the third *Carabinieri*, Diego, having realized following orders would get him nowhere, decided to own the law, so he argued with the *Carabinieri* in an authoritarian tone of voice: "There

was no fair warning … I am transporting my elderly mother, etc."
The *Carabinieri* subsequently turned his back to Diego, making him
even angrier to be dissed in such a fashion, until he realized that
it was the *Carabinieri's* way of ceding the law to him and inviting
him to drive right on through. Can you imagine this happening
in the United States?

Moving Tourists

Moving tourists around Rome has become a creative art. In
addition to these new Segway tours, I've noticed a number of bike
tours, which I had never noticed in Rome before. What helped
catalyze these bike tours? The establishment of a short-term, urban
bike rental system, according to Diego. I had noticed a couple sets
of rental bike racks during my exploratory walks, but they were
all empty, which I thought was odd. According to Diego, Roman
entrepreneurs have more or less taken control of these municipali-
ty-funded racks using the bikes to give tours. What a fine example
of Italian-style (and increasingly US-style?) capitalism, private
entrepreneurs making a profit off the government.

Old-fashioned walking tours, with umbrella-toting leaders,
still abound, though now with personalized audio systems to facil-
itate listening. And of course, the double-decker bus tours. I took
one of these soon after I arrived to get a sense of Rome's layout,
only to abort the ride prematurely when, all of a sudden, there was
a mini-explosion. One of the tires blew.

Recycling Roman-Style

Rome has embraced recycling, I think. One of the only points
the owner of my apartment emphasized when I arrived was the
importance of separating my trash. In the kitchen are four sets of
trashcans with different-colored bags for each type of trash: paper,
organic, non-recyclable, and a fourth mystery category. Based on
the directions of my apartment owner and on the complicated,

color-coded recycling direction sheet on the front door of my building, I am still uncertain as to what is considered recyclable.

Making things even more complicated, I can never remember which day I am allowed to put out which type of trash. Each day of the week is designated for a different type of trash pick-up. And, according to the rules, one is supposed to put out the trash between 7:00 a.m. and 8:30 a.m. I often leave after 8:30 a.m., and given the seventy-three-step altitude of my apartment, I haven't been eager to make special trash trips, so I started to accumulate trash. Until one day I noticed when leaving my apartment at 10:30 a.m., trash bags were still sitting outside all the front doors in the neighborhood. Phew, some added window time there.

To further dispel the rigidity of Italian law, Diego dismissively remarked that recycling in Rome is nothing but a charade. All the trash goes to the same place. After all the thought and diligence that I had been exerting properly separating my four categories of trash, I chose not to believe him. Until I actually saw my first trash pick-up operation live this past week with the trash guy throwing various colored-coded trash bags all into the same truck. I chose to believe that these bags are painstakingly separated at their final destination.

Sad Economics

On a more pessimistic note, I just read Frank Bruni's October 26, 2013, *New York Times* editorial, "Italy Breaks Your Heart," which rings true to me with respect to the dismal job market and dysfunctional political situation. What he doesn't mention are Italy's scary demographics, which further cloud its future. Italy's fertility rate currently is only 1.4, having hovered between 1.2 and 1.4 since the late 1980s. The US rate has hovered between 1.9 and 2.1 (replacement rate) since 1970. Europe's demographic meltdown is a critical issue with profound implications, most of them bad.

The owner of my apartment, a former management consultant, is fairly critical of Italy's political and economic situation and highly recommended that I read a *Corriere della Serra* editorial published this past Thursday, October 24, 2013, by two political economists who have taught at Harvard and MIT, "A country in decline is one that crowds out those who are productive." Instead of dividing Italy up between north and south, they draw a line of delineation between Italians who are producing world-class exportable products and those who are thwarting this productive activity through cronyism, excessive bureaucracy/rules/labor rigidity, and the lack of a well-functioning capital market. I think it is spot on.

It seems that thoughtful folks in Europe and the United States increasingly understand clearly our current challenges and constructive solutions, but our respective political systems have degenerated to a point that renders them incapable of addressing the problems. The question of *why* our political systems have become so dysfunctional is one that I personally think requires more discussion.

Father Diego says Rome is a city of takers as opposed to producers, with its funding dependent on tourists, government, and the church. From what I have seen so far, I can't argue with this assessment, though, as a Romanized tourist, I cannot complain.

Ciao di Roma

DISPATCH 8

"Halloween" Roman-Style

This has been a long holiday weekend in Italy. In New York City, the weekend was marked by Halloween celebrations and the wonderful marathon, which I dearly missed. Here in Rome, we have been commemorating all the saints (November 1) and souls (November 2) who preceded us on this earth. Worldfund's first employee, and now friend, visited me these past few days, allowing me to play Roman tour guide for the first time.

On the top of our to-do list was a visit to the church, Santa Maria della Concezione dei Cappuccini, known for its elaborate, if not macabre, decorations incorporating the bones of some four thousand Capuchin Friars. The Capuchin Friars are a branch of the Franciscan order, which Francis of Assisi founded in 1209. The church, located in a fairly swanky neighborhood on Via Veneto, right down the street from the US Embassy, is undergoing a major restoration, so we were only able to explore the half dozen crypts below the church, which have been converted into a museum.

My two favorite crypts were the "Pelvis bone crypt" and the "Thigh and leg bone crypt." Some find the Catholic Church's tradition of venerating relics curious, if not morbid. For those of us in modern, highly developed economies, where death is not an in-your-face part of daily life, a focus on death can be unsettling. Being within touching distance of so many bones was certainly unsettling for me. But I also found the experience edifying and yes, life affirming, which I believe was the aim of the crypt bone artisans who worked on the crypts between 1500 and 1870. There is nothing like seeing the finish line to prioritize and motivate.

A Visit to Purgatory

One would think a church known for its Piccolo Museo del Purgatorio would be open all day on All Souls Day (November 2). Nope. Church visiting hours were 8:30 till 11:30 a.m. and again from 4:30 to 6:30 p.m. We arrived to Sacro Cuore di Gesu—located right around the corner from the beautiful Piazza Cavour in the tony Prati neighborhood—at 4:35, joining a small group of folks, including a few nuns and priests, waiting for the man with the key to open the door. With zero haste, the key man opened the doors. Upon entering, with my finally attuned tourism antennae, I noticed an Italian man making his way quickly to the front right corner of the church. We followed closely on his heels, and sure enough, he walked right into a small side room where on a single wall hung about ten frames, which included scraps of paper and fabrics, each with either burnt-looking handprints or fingerprints.

A booklet of typed stories explained the contents of each of the ten frames. Frame 5 contained: "A photo of the mark made by the deceased Mrs. Leleux, on the sleeve of her son Joseph's shirt, when she appeared to him on the night of 21 June 1789 at Wodecq, Belgium. The son related that for a period of eleven consecutive nights, he had heard noises, which almost made him sick with fear …"

According to the booklet explanation of frame 5, the deceased Mrs. Leleux reminded her son of his duty to attend Mass, per his father's will. She also chided him for his dissolute way of life and begged him to repent and do good works for the church. Joseph took his deceased mother's warnings seriously, converted, and founded a religious congregation before his death in 1825.

By the time we exited the room, there was a long line of folks waiting to get in.

Some More Fantastic Church Art

I took my friend to see the two Caravaggio paintings I so love in Santa Maria del Popolo. Unlike me, she travels with a smartphone and looked up what else might be of interest in the church. Wouldn't you know? There are two wonderful Bernini statues that I had missed, located near the entrance of the church in the Chigi Chapel, *Habakkuk and the Angel* and *Daniel and the Lion*.

Earlier in the week, I unexpectedly happened upon another Caravaggio located in the beautiful Chiesa Sant'Agostino, slightly north of the Pantheon and Piazza Navona. I had never seen or heard of this minor basilica, which holds the remains of St. Monica, the long-suffering mother of the great St. Augustine.

In the first chapel on the left when you enter is Caravaggio's *Madonna dei Pellegrini*. Like all his works, it is a masterpiece of composition, light, color, and realistic detail. While I did not care for how Caravaggio portrayed the Madonna's stance, I was struck by how he painted her right hand grasping at baby Jesus, exactly as Michelangelo did in the Pieta.

Fantastic Private Art Collections

Over the past ten days, I visited two delightful family-run, private collections—Palazzo Colonna and Palazzo Daria Pamphilj. Both are housed in palaces of prominent, old Roman families, each boasting their own family pope: Pope Oddone Colonna (1417–1431) and Pope Innocent X (Pamphilj) (1644–1655).

The Palazzo Colonna did not have as many major works as the Daria Pamphilj, but the tasteful opulence of the palace was stunning. Of the massive art collection, which covered all the wall space of nearly all the rooms, I was most struck by three large, unusual, and modern-looking paintings by an artist I had never heard of, Ridolfo del Ghirandaio (Florence, 1483–1561)—*Venere e Amore, La Notte,* and *Aurora.*

What I loved most about my Daria Pamphilj visit was the

taped tour, recorded by a direct descendent of the family, Jonathan Pamphilj. There are a number of Brits who married into the Pamphilj family, which I think may explain the family's more civ-ic-oriented mind-set, that of being stewards of a great collection that must be well maintained and made available to the public. Jonathan speaks with a beautiful British accent and recounts personal family stories about growing up in the palazzo, including one in which he and his sister found themselves in big trouble for roller-skating on the beautiful old terrazzo floors of one of the grand salons.

The fantastic Pamphilj collection, which is better organized and better signed than the Palazzo Colonna, includes two Caravaggios and a stunning Velasquez portrait of Pope Innocent. For those who love the Frick Museum, they would also really love the Daria Pamphilj and the Palazzo Colonna. I also plan to visit three other privately run villa collections–Palazzo Farnese (now the French Embassy), Galleria Borghese (located in the Villa Borghese), and Villa Farnesina, which is very close to my apartment.

Some Sacred Music

This is a big week on the music front, as I plan to attend a number of concerts, which are part of the Twelfth Annual International Festival of Sacred Music. I worked hard at securing a place. After careful study of the website, I figured out that one could only secure seating at this series of nine concerts if one is a benefactor of the Sacred Music Foundation, so I made a donation. Success! I subsequently received an email inviting me to pick up a special badge at an office near the Vatican granting me entrance to all the concerts.

I attended my first concert of the series last night, and I will never forget it! Held at the beautiful Basilica di Santa Maria Maggiore, where Pope Francis snuck out to pray the morning after he was named pope, the program included the Moscow Synodal Choir and the Pontifical Sistine Chapel Choir. My three favorite pieces of the evening were sung by the Russian choir and were absolutely beautiful!

- Traditional Slavic Christmas song, "*Ot Junosti Mojeja*" ("From my Youth")
- Georgy Swiridov (1915–1998), "*Ljubov Svjataja*" ("Sacred Love")
- Hilarion Alfeyev (b. 1966, Russian Orthodox Bishop): "*Vo Tzarstvii Tvoem*" ("In Your Kingdom")

Ciao di Roma

DISPATCH 9

Just as I was starting to slip into that deadened routine zone where, during one's daily activities, thinking crowds out observation, I was thrust again into Roman tour-guide mode. Some New York City friends came to visit for a week, staying in a beautiful, peaceful converted convent hotel, Hotel Donna Camilla Savelli, right around the corner from my own peaceful apartment.

Mozzarella

I have tended to eat at restaurants only when invited by new Roman friends, or with visitors, so this afforded me an entire week of nonstop restaurant eating. One of our more memorable meals was at Due Ladroni, recommended by a close friend back home but closed on my first visit. True to its online reviews, the food was fabulous, the service terrific, and the (other) customers beautiful but low-key. It is the first restaurant I have been to so far in Rome that focuses on fish and does it very well.

Despite the great fish choices, I could not resist one of my all-time favorite food combinations. For my *primo plato*, I ordered a plate of *mozzarella di bufalo* and prosciutto. Fantastic! While I had already enjoyed some of the best-tasting mozzarella I had ever eaten, purchased at a small *salumeria* in Trastevere, I had never tasted prosciutto so tender and flavorful. It is a mystery to me why the rubber balls called mozzarella sold in American supermarkets have the same name as the soft, gooey-inside, a-touch-pungent delight sold here in Italy.

Mozzarella originates in Campania, near Naples. The best is made from the milk of buffalo, as opposed to cows, and the first known mention of mozzarella comes from a late sixteenth-century cookbook. According to the Mozzarella di Bufala trade association, cited in Wikipedia:

> The cheese-maker kneads it with his hands, like a baker making bread, until he obtains a smooth, shiny paste, a strand of which he pulls out and lops off, forming the individual mozzarella. It is then typically formed into ball shapes or in plait. In Italy, a 'rubbery' consistency is generally considered not satisfactory; the cheese is expected to be softer.

Borghese Gallery: Fantastic Art, Miserably Managed Museum

The four highlights from my New York City friends' stay in Rome were visits to the Borghese Gallery, the Scavi, a guided tour of the Vatican Museum/Sistine Chapel, and a music concert. All required advanced planning and were well worth the effort.

The ground floor of the Borghese Gallery is spectacular from an architectural and sculptural point of view. I have never studied architecture or interior design. Nonetheless, the beauty and harmony of the former Baroque-style villa of the Borghese family makes a strong impression on even a neophyte. There is a lot going on, but it all fits together so perfectly. In one main room, the color scheme, embodied in an array of different materials, is made up of golden oranges, pinks, and a touch of green. If someone had told me that pink and orange could look fantastic together, I never would have believed it before seeing the Borghese Gallery. And the sculptures, many Bernini, are otherworldly. The upstairs painting galleries were interesting but not as arresting as the downstairs.

What made a big, negative impression on my three New York City friends and me was how extraordinarily dysfunctional the check-in process was and how rude the staff were. Entering and exiting the gallery required five separate lines in one tiny space with a single entry-exit door, minimal signage, and even less help from the museum staff.

Having lived in Budapest in the 1980s, the Borghese Gallery visit prompted memories of the lines and attitudes I experienced in communist Hungary. It is unconscionable that the experience of viewing such an extraordinary treasure is undermined by such ineptness and indifference. To top it off, the tickets and recorder guide, which explained only a small handful of the paintings, cost US$25, so relative to other Roman sites, no bargain.

I had assumed the Borghese Gallery was privately owned and managed, like the Galleria Doria Pamphilj or Palazzo Colonna. Accordingly, I was baffled as to why this most important 'private' gallery was run so poorly. In fact, the Borghese Gallery was sold to the Italian government in 1902. And sure enough, upon a quick search, one notices that the gallery is part of the Italian government's arts website. I write this with a thread of hope that someone who can make a difference may eventually read this.

Scavi and the Bones of St. Peter

In contrast, our Scavi visit represented the height of organization and professionalism. The Roman Catholic Church definitely has something over the Italian government when it comes to moving crowds and making accessible its treasures. Right on the dot at 1:45 p.m., our fantastic Hungarian tour guide greeted us and guided us through the Scavi (tombs) under St. Peter's Basilica. (I am compelled to make a positive observation about a county I also love, Hungary.) There is so much to say about the Scavi, and one truly must experience it to fully appreciate their importance.

A few memorable notes: The current St. Peter's (construction begun in 1506 and took over one hundred years to complete) is the second basilica built on the site. In the fourth century, Emperor Constantine built the first basilica on a hill that served as a burial ground for both pagans and Christians. At the foot of this hill, where St. Peter's Square now stands, was a Roman circus, in the middle of which was erected the large obelisk that still stands today in the square.

St. Peter was crucified upside down in this square in AD 64, possibly looking at the very same obelisk that is there today. Early Christian faithful buried St. Peter's bones in this hill above the circus in a vaguely marked spot so as to protect the sacred bones during an era of brutal persecution under Nero. The main altar of the first, and now second, basilica are located directly above where St Peter's bones, wrapped in a cloth and placed in a simple box, were buried. Scientific discovery verified this long-held legend of St. Peter's bones only in recent years.

Pope Pius XII, a man who had a great appreciation for archeology, sanctioned five renowned archeologists to secretly work under St. Peter's Basilica for ten years from the late 1930s through WWII. Can you imagine? A secret dig under St. Peter's in the middle of one of the most brutal wars in history! The archeologists discovered a number of Christian burial spots, but they could not identify the particular bones of St. Peter with any certainty.

In 1953 Italian archeologist Margherita Guarducci identified the burial box containing St. Peter's bones, which had been secretly moved in 1942 by a monsignor, ignorant of archeological practices, for safekeeping. In 1968, Pope Paul VI announced to the world that, with great certainty, they had found St. Peter's bones.

Vatican Tour Guide Extraordinaire, Liz Lev

Like the Scavi tour, words do not do justice to our three-hour tour of the Vatican Museum and Sistine Chapel led by art historian-"theologian" tour guide extraordinaire Liz Lev. She makes art and architecture come alive and speak to us as if they were living people. You will have to go on one of her tours to learn why Noah and Jonah were such important prophets and how this is conveyed in early Christian artwork and in Michelangelo's very own Sistine Chapel ceiling paintings.

There is too much to see in the Vatican collection in one week, let alone in one day. What Liz does is identify a few seminal pieces and focuses intensely on these from an artistic, historic, sociological, and theological perspective. I mention only one here. After quickly shepherding us through the Vatican Museum lobby housing an inexplicably awful collection of modern work, Liz started our tour with *Laocoon and His Sons*. This fantastic, Baroque-like statue is Hellenistic—a style that developed in Greek Asia Minor around 200 BC—but was excavated near Rome in 1506. According to Liz, this statue was a critically important inspiration for Michelangelo's Sistine Chapel figures and is one of the most important works in the Vatican collection.

A Concert for East-West Unity

For our last evening, we attended a wonderful concert organized by Robert Moynihan, a veteran Vatican reporter who recently started a foundation to encourage closer Eastern Orthodox and Roman Catholic relations. Performed were a couple of works composed by the same Russian Orthodox bishop, Metropolitan Hilarian Alfeyev, whose pieces I had been impressed by at the concert I attended and wrote about at the Basilica Santa Maria sopra Minerva. Metropolitan Hilarian Alfeyev attended the concert, along with a handful of cardinals.

We were happy that our seats were not directly behind the Russian Orthodox bishop, as he was wearing a large white headpiece, a major view-blocker. I would love to learn the formal name of this headpiece. I do not think it is called a *mitre*, the elaborate headpiece that the pope and Eastern Orthodox bishops wear during high Masses.

A Gelato and Movie Ending

I recently discovered, and brought my friends to, arguably the best gelato place in Rome—Gelateria del Teatro. I could not find their website, but this review on the Trevor Morrow travel website is one I agree with wholeheartedly: "And while Rome is full of gelato shops (many of which dish out air-filled, uninspired, and overpriced gelato) Stefano's Gelateria del Teatro is a shining, unique, sincere, and refreshing beacon of culinary hope. It's a place where gelato turns into little cups of art, and merely satisfying your sweet tooth turns into a travel experience to remember."

I admit to four visits thus far, my favorite flavor being Sicilian Almond. My tighter-fitting jeans are not happy so I will have to enter a penitential no-pasta-wine-gelato-mozzarella phase.

On an ending note, in today's *NYTimes* I read a movie review of *The Great Beauty*, a film set in current-day Rome. Whereas in many of Woody Allen's earlier movies New York City was a central character, Rome is the central character in *The Great Beauty*. The opening scene was filmed only blocks from my apartment—on the Jeniculum Hill, at Fontana dell'Acqua Paola, which I am looking up upon as I write these words.

Ciao di Roma

DISPATCH 10

La Scala

I've left Rome twice since my late September arrival, both times to northern Italy—Milan and Bologna, where I lived for a year twenty-five years ago as a student. I was able to make both trips in a single day, thanks to the Euro $150 billion that was invested in six hundred miles of special tracks and tunnels from Turin all the way down to Naples to support new speed trains. I used to remember it taking some 3.5 hours to get from Bologna to Rome. Now it only takes just under two hours.

Naples—where I plan to visit after Christmas and where my mother warned me not to try the mozzarella thanks to a distressing November 25, 2013, *WSJ* article titled, "Naples's Garbage Crisis Piles Up on City Outskirts: Toxic Bonfires Fuel Mounting Concerns About Contaminated Food and Water"—is only one hour by train from Rome now.

Thanks to the generosity and efforts of the Milanese grandfather of one of Worldfund's Mexican IAPE staff (who also drilled me in Italian during an intensive course I took at Dartmouth this past summer), I had a middle orchestra section seat at La Scala a week ago Sunday for the performance of *Aida*. It will go down as one of my most memorable experiences here in Italy.

I hadn't realized how intimate La Scala is, much smaller than the New York Metropolitan Opera. The size of the venue and strength of the singers—a largely Russian/Ukraine cast, including a fantastic Liudmyla Monastyrska as Aida—made it feel as if the music was pulsing right through you. Always comparing and contrasting, seeing Liudmyla Monastyrska on stage made me realize that one very infrequently sees really large sopranos at the

Met these days under Peter Gelb, who tends to emphasize acting, dance, and the ascetic elements of opera perhaps a bit more than traditional managers.

I also noticed that La Scala's season had many fewer performances (I counted just over one hundred performances of ten operas) than the Met (which had 209 performances of twenty-eight operas last year). Most, if not all, of the Scala's program were from the traditional repertoire and mostly Verdi during this hundred-anniversary Verdi year. While not as "out there" as German opera houses, the Met seems to take more artistic risks than La Scala.

My financial analyst left brain started rearing its head, and I became curious about budgets and funding. Very telling differences! More than one-third of La Scala's 2012 budget of US$157 million came from government funding, the rest mostly from ticket sales. Some US$6.75 million of government funding was cut this year (to help pay for the debt on the six hundred miles of railroad tracks?), which forced a reduction in the number of performances. By contrast, the Met budget in 2012 was US$325 million, with a whopping US$182 million raised from private donations. Less than 2 percent of the Met's budget is funded by government grants.

A Milanese Way of Celebrating Mass

I had been to Milan twice, on brief marketing trips when I was a sell-side analyst. Quite unexpectedly, I walked by the offices of one of the banking firms I visited, located right behind the Scala. Little did I realize fifteen years ago where I was. It was all work no play back then. I attended Mass at the Duomo di Milano and discovered that the Catholic Church has an Ambrosian (or Milanese) Rite, which differs from the Roman Rite that most American and European Catholics are used to.

When the priest walked out in the purple vestments of Advent, I literally looked at my calendar to see if it was already Advent, which starts four Sundays before Christmas. Parts of the Mass were said in a different order than a normal Mass that I was used to. I sat in the pews thinking this priest was making a slew of liturgical mistakes. This baffled me, being at the cathedral where I would have thought these priests would have known better.

Every Roman Rite Mass, no matter where you are in the world, uses the same prayers in the same order, so normally there are few surprises (apart from music quality and the odd thing or two a priest may throw in the homily). It turns out the Ambrosian Rite celebrates six weeks of Advent. The history behind why the 5 million or so Catholics in the Milan area celebrate the Ambrosian Rite is beyond me to recount, but Wikipedia provides a very detailed explanation.

The greatest overall impression I came away with from my ten-hour visit to Milan was that it was a city going places, productive, full of energy, lots of construction—unlike Rome. I love Rome as a visitor. But Rome is a museum as compared to Milan. Milan feels almost Germanic, and indeed, I was told that the people of Lombardy (which produces one-fifth of Italy's GDP and is one of the richest regions in all of Europe) are more similar to Germans than to Roman Italians. If stop sign behavior is any proof, then I absolutely believe it. In front of La Scala there is a four-way, low-traffic intersection with stoplights. Despite no cars coming from any direction and the light remaining red forever, no one crossed the street until the light turned green. It reminded me of the German tourists I see in NYC waiting for the green walk light while literally every New Yorker walks right by them, sometimes right in front of a car with the right of way.

Bologna and Mother Theresa

I had not been back to Bologna since my stay there as a student in the late 1980s. I have such fond memories of the city. Normally I find one builds up positive memories such that the reality, when revisited, often falls short. Incredibly, my seven-hour or so stay in Bologna exceeded my expectations, despite the rain and cold that greeted me. Bologna is an arcaded city, so not a bad place to be in the rain. Below is the only iPad photo I shot that day, of an arcaded section of Via Santo Stefano leading to my apartment.

Basilica Santo Stefano, Bologna

Living in Bologna as a student, I regularly walked by the Basilica Santo Stefano complex, part of which dates back to the eighth century. One of my most vivid memories of my year in Bologna was a talk given by Mother Teresa in this very square. What struck me was how adamantly she spoke out against abortion. As hard as this may be to believe, it was the first time I had heard such a heartfelt defense of life. I was able to find a YouTube minute video of Mother Teresa accepting, in English, some sort of honor bestowed on her in Bologna on September 26, 1987, which clearly was the reason she came to Bologna.

As with Milan, Bologna has a very different feel from Rome, with a very orderly, sophisticated, intellectual, clean design. And the food. Bologna is the gastronomic capital of Italy! I brought back to Rome a bag of homemade tortellini that I subsequently prepared with olive oil and a bit of Romano cheese. Delectable. Bologna is worth a trip just for the homemade tortellini.

Various Tidbits

A dear friend visited me this past weekend, on the way back from a business trip to London. Despite two days of pouring rain, with a brief respite when she took the attached photo of me in Piazza Navona (one of my favorite piazzas), we thoroughly enjoyed ourselves. I had arranged another Vatican Museum tour with the fantastic Liz Lev. I have visited the museum and Sistine Chapel a number of times now, and each time is as powerful as the last. The extraordinary beauty of the artwork and architecture screams out.

Me in my favorite Piazza Navona

Three new and unforgettable tastes I experienced this past week were *ricotta al forno di limone*, limoncello made with pistachio, and *sfogliatelle*. I have tried sfogliatelle from Arthur Avenue, Bronx, and Little Italy, Boston, and none compared to the one I purchased here at a bakery near Campo di Fiori. I had never before tried *ricotta al forno di limone*, sweetened ricotta with lemon, eaten as a dessert—delectable. In the Campo Fiori daily market, a certain vender sells about ten flavors of limoncello, which he invites the curious to sample. I made a beeline for the pistachio and absolutely loved it.

I was asked to give a talk at the Acton Institute of Rome this past Thursday on the topic of "Human Capital" as it relates to the Catholic understanding of the person and to economic development. It gave me an opportunity to read the pope's encyclicals on work and the economy—*Rerum Novarum* (1891), *Laborem Exercens* (1981), and *Centesimus Annus* (1991)—which are fantastic. They reflect a profound understanding of how the economy works and man's place in the economy.

I wish you all a wonderful Thanksgiving. I certainly have a lot to be thankful for this year.

Ciao di Roma

DISPATCH 11

In Search of our Family Saint ...

I set out early Saturday morning for Otranto, where Capitano Francesco Zurlo, a descendent of our family according to my father's genealogy work, was martyred on August 14, 1480. Otranto is a walled town on the easternmost tip of the Italian boot heel. One can actually see Albania (though not Russia) from the shore of Otranto. The trip from Rome to Otranto, via Lecce, entailed trains, buses, walking, and many inquiries extended to skeptical Italians who doubted the feasibility of a round trip to Otranto in a New Yorker's time frame.

... Via Lecce

Italy's train system has done nothing but impress me. Every train I have taken so far has left exactly on time. I left Rome's Termini station at 8:05 a.m. and arrived in Lecce at just before two in the afternoon to pouring rain. My window for exploring this extraordinary city was very limited, so I stuck out the never-ending downpour and explored the city center as the beautiful limestone streets started flooding.

During a rest break at an empty bar right across from the beautiful duomo, the owner frustratingly explained that we were in the middle of a Neptune storm and that it would continue like this for the next two days. Normally Lecce is packed with both locals and tourists strolling the extraordinarily beautiful streets. This evening I had Lecce virtually to myself.

Some call Lecce the Florence of the south. It is a small Baroque city *par excellence* filled with spectacular churches. Whereas Roman churches tend to be undistinguished on the exterior and extraordinary inside, Lecce's churches are gorgeous inside and out. Lecce's aesthetic claim to fame is the sublimely sculpted limestone making up the beautiful Baroque-to-the-hilt facades and altars of Lecce's many churches and public buildings.

To the left of the main altar of the Basilica di Santa Croce is beautiful painting that depicts the vegan, animal-lover saint, Francis di Paola (1416–1506), named after the more famous St. Francis of Assisi. St. Francis di Paola had the gift of prophecy and predicted the Turkish invasion of Otranto. The limestone carved altar depicts many scenes of his life and prophecies, including the Otranto invasion itself.

The owner of the bed and breakfast I stayed at suggested that I not trust the Internet Otranto bus schedule. So I returned to the train station, which also serves as a bus station, to check on times in person. Once there and after many inquiries, I found a remote office at the end of one of the train track platforms where a very friendly ticket agent shook his head when I asked about Sunday round-trip tickets to Otranto. After some checking he discovered that indeed I could get to Otranto and back in one day via a connection in some town along the way. The total round-trip cost for the eighty-kilometer round trip—Euro$7! A deal!

I woke up Sunday morning to an unexpected surprise: sun! My experience with Italian weather predictions is that they are almost always wrong. Like the Italian trains, the bus to Otranto took off right on time. But it did not arrive on time to my connection town, as we were held up for some thirty minutes for a road race held in the middle of a tiny town called Zollino.

I had always been struck by the number of Italians jogging about NYC leading up to the NYC Marathon. I had not fully appreciated Italy's running culture until seeing this rather large road race in a tiny town in Italy's boot heel. Thankfully, the connecting bus waited for us, and twenty minutes later I arrived to a deserted train/bus station outside Otranto's walled center.

Otranto's history extends back to BC times, largely determined by its critical strategic location. Only in Spain have I seen the walls of ancient towns in such great shape. However, the great walls were not able to thwart the Turks from overtaking this strategically important town in 1480.

On July 28, 1480, Muhammed II sent Gedik Achmet Pascia and eighteen thousand Turkish soldiers to conquer Otranto as a southern foothold for the Turks' European expansion aims. The six thousand citizens of Otranto and soldiers of King Alfonso of Aragon, led by Francesco Zurlo, held off the Turks for fifteen days, until August 12, when the Turks were able to break through the city walls.

According to the pamphlet I picked up at the basilica of Otranto, "Captains Francesco Zurlo and Giannantonio Delli Falconi fell heroically while trying to contain the enemy attack." According to my father, Capitano Francesco Zurlo was cut in half at the stomach.

According to some Internet research:

Francesco Zurlo, Lord of Pietragallo, Oppido, Casalaspro, Atisciano and Brittoli, belonged to the aristocratic branch of the Apulian Piscicelli Neapolitan family who had adopted the name Zurlo, widespread fish in the sea of Otranto, to stand out from the original branch. The chronicle of the family is recorded since ancient times and has enjoyed, with mixed success, nobility in Naples and in Salento.

I surmise that the "mixed success" is what led my great-grandfather to come to America. I am proud to say that we also have our requisite family cardinal Cardinal Giuseppe Maria Capece Zurlo, 1711–1801.

Two days after the Turks killed Zurlo and Falconi, on August 14, they rounded up eight hundred men of Otranto over the age of fifteen and ordered them to renounce their Christian faith and convert to Islam. Led by Antonio Primaldo, a tailor, they all refused and were beheaded on Colle della Minerva, the hill next to Otranto. Legend has it that Primaldo was the first to be beheaded and remained standing throughout the entire slaughter.

Thirteen months after the slaughter, King Alfonso retook Otranto, gathered up the eight hundred bodies, which were left unburied on the hill, and had 560 of them placed in the Otranto Basilica, photo below, and 240 brought to Naples, where they are now venerated in Chiesa di Santa Catarina a Formiello. The Otranto Basilica, built in the eleventh century, is also famous for its remarkably preserved floor mosaic depicting the history of man from the fall of Adam to the resurrection.

Heads of Otranto martyrs

On October 5, 1980, Pope John Paul II visited Otranto to celebrate Mass on the five hundredth anniversary of the martyrdom. On July 5, 2007, JPII beatified the eight hundred martyrs, and on February 11, 2013, Pope Benedict XVI declared them saints during the same address in which he announced his historic decision to step down as pope. On May 13, 2013, Pope Francis I canonized the eight hundred martyrs of Otranto, including Francesco Zurlo. It was a touching experience to spend the day in this beautiful, historic town, which is very proud of its storied history. One highlight among many was seeing a street sign with our family name.

A Visit to Padre Pio

I woke up early yesterday morning (Monday) and caught a train north to Foggia. As for the other half of my Italian side, my great-grandfather was born in Foggia. His name was Comincio di Goia, derived from the verb *cominciare*, meaning to begin, as he was the first and only boy born after a gaggle of girls. From Foggia I took a one-hour bus ride east to San Giovanni Rotondo, home of Saint Padre Pio, until his death in 1968.

Padre Pio led an extraordinarily holy life and suffered from the stigmata starting in 1911. His body lies incorrupt in the tomb of a newly erected church designed by Renzo Piano, next to the original church and attached apartment where he lived and served as priest. The mosaics in and around the tomb chapel are spectacular. San Giovanni Rotondo receives some 8 million pilgrims a year—versus 5 million for Lourdes and 3 million for Fatima and 12 million for the Basilica of Guadalupe. It was another chilly, somewhat rainy day, and I virtually had the pilgrimage site to myself, which I was thankful for.

Padre Pio incorrupt

At 5:30 p.m. I boarded a bus to Rome and arrived home at about eleven in the evening to see my street beautifully decorated with Christmas lights! Rome is bursting with Christmas decorations and activity. Italy at Christmastime is very special.

Ciao di Roma

DISPATCH 12

Pope Francis's First Major Communiqué

Pope Francis's *Evangelii Gaudium*, published last week, has received much attention from Catholics and non-Catholics alike. Traditionally, a new pope's first major communiqué provides a window into how the pope will orient his pontificate. With unprecedented speed, Pope Francis captured the hearts of world, so it is understandable why his words are being so carefully perused. A number of you have asked my opinion of *Evangelii Gaudium*, a daunting task, but here goes.

Evangelii Gaudium (*The Joy of the Gospel*) is an apostolic exhortation divided into five chapters. An apostolic exhortation is a form of papal communication that is lower in teaching authority than a papal encyclical and generally targets a broader audience than Catholic bishops alone. Reflective of Pope Francis's style, the language is informal. But unlike Pope Francis's relatively brief speaking style, the exhortation is long, 216 pages in English, a bit wordy such that it would have benefitted from more editing.

In terms of subject matter, it is pure Francis through and through—a passionate appeal to Catholics to joyfully live their faith and reach out to others proclaiming God's infinite love for us. I was touched by the power and beauty of many, many passages. Pope Francis is first and foremost an evangelizer. I think this is exactly what our world needs right now—an authentic, hopeful messenger who is able to touch the hearts of many, especially those who are not currently close to the church.

Pope Francis devotes a long section to specific, caring advice toward priests, including how long a homily should be and how many points it should have (a Jesuitical three). This is in response to his Latin American experience, where the Catholic Church continues to lose people to Evangelical and Pentecostal sects due to poor pastoral care by too many priests. Pope Francis views his primary function as that of a pastor, and he expects his priests to do so too.

The sections that are getting the most attention are the ones that speak about the poor, and like Mother Theresa, Pope Francis is not referring just to the materially poor but also to the spiritually poor. This opening paragraph describes beautifully what Francis views as one of the great tragedies and challenges in today's world.

> 2. The great danger in today's world, pervaded as it is by consumerism, is the desolation and anguish born of a complacent yet covetous heart, the feverish pursuit of frivolous pleasures, and a blunted conscience. Whenever our interior life becomes caught up in its own interests and concerns, there is no longer room for others, no place for the poor. God's voice is no longer heard, the quiet joy of his love is no longer felt, and the desire to do good fades.

Pope Francis potently criticizes two elements of today's global economic system: an undue focus on satisfying unquenchable consumerism and an obsessive focus on profits at the expense of people. He also speaks passionately about the many who can't even participate in the economy due to a lack of skills—a challenge that many of you are trying to address and understand all too well how difficult this is to do.

> 53. "Human beings are themselves considered consumer goods to be used and then discarded. We have created a "throw away" culture, which is now spreading. It is no longer simply about exploitation and oppression, but something new. Exclusion ultimately has to do with what it means to be a part of the society in which we live; those excluded are no longer society's underside or its fringes or

its disenfranchised—they are no longer even a part of it. The excluded are not the "exploited" but the outcast, the 'leftovers'.

Many consider Pope Emeritus Benedict to be one of the most intellectually brilliant of all popes. His first encyclical, *Deus Caritas Est* (*God Is Love*, 2005) is truly extraordinary for its profound insights and beautiful, precise prose. I had the opportunity to attend a small Mass offered by the then Cardinal Ratzinger, in March 2003 and found him to be gentle and humble—attributes that are exceedingly rare in a powerful and brilliant person. I believe that Pope Benedict XVI was greatly misunderstood by the broader world. This misunderstanding, combined with his introverted, intellectual bent, may have limited his ability to evangelize in today's world.

Pope Francis, in contrast, is an extroverted man of the heart, and as such, he is resonating better among broader audiences. How hungry the world is for an authentic leader who publicly lives out the message of truth and love. Words have become cheap in today's hyper-communicated world, increasing the importance of lived example. This is why Pope Francis's external simplicity and shows of real affection and love are so attractive.

Pope Francis connects with others on a down-to-earth, heart-to-heart level as a means of communicating the gospel message, relying less on formal language. Indeed, during the four times I have observed Pope Francis addressing large audiences in St. Peter's Square, he could not help himself from looking up from his prepared script and speaking directly from his heart. These were the words that were the most touching and evoked the most fervent reaction. These were transcendent moments.

Pope Francis's word choice related to two short passages about the economy, unfortunately, has overshadowed *Evangelii Gaudium*'s main message.

54. Some people continue to defend trickle-down theories which assume that economic growth, encouraged by a free market, will inevitably succeed in bringing about greater justice and inclusiveness in the world. This opinion, which has never been confirmed by the facts, expresses a crude and naïve trust in the goodness of those wielding economic power ...

56. While the earnings of a minority are growing exponentially, so too is the gap separating the majority from the prosperity enjoyed by those happy few. This imbalance is the result of ideologies, which defend the absolute autonomy of the marketplace and financial speculation. Consequently, they reject the right of states, charged with vigilance for the common good, to exercise any form of control

Some have blamed faulty translations from the pope's native Spanish. The translation does obfuscate the underlying meaning a bit, but it does not fully explain a more critical treatment of capitalism, particularly relative to a more benign treatment of state power, especially in its overarching or corrupt manifestations.

Before trying to explain this difference in emphasis, it is important to note that the political economy question is less important to Pope Francis than individual attitudes (explained well in the first cited quote), which are at the root of injustices perpetrated against the poor. Pope Francis is not a liberation theologian in a Marxist sense as some would have us believe.

The gospel is full of paradox. I believe one of the great strengths of the Catholic Church, played out through the ages, is her ability to synthesize and speak to the paradoxical nature of our human condition and of God. Indeed, Pope Francis himself writes, "Where your synthesis is, there lies your heart" (para. 143). Debates and tensions amongst theologians, priests, and lay faithful often hinge on emphasis and on the ideal balance between two seemingly incompatible extremes.

Ever since the Pope Leo XIII's momentous Encyclical, *Rerum Novarum* (1891), the church has spoken eloquently about the common good, lauding the benefits of a market economy while at the same time warning against its potential pitfalls as they relate to personal well-being, especially of the poor and weak. *Rerum Novarum*, and its two updates, *Laborem Exercens* (1981) and *Centesimus Annus* (1991), are fairly balanced with respect to the attendant evils that both an unregulated free market economy and an over-arching state can potentially unleash due to their intrinsic natures.

Evangelii Gaudium does not elaborate upon broader society and the common good as much as these earlier three encyclicals, but in its brief diagnosis of the structural causes of poverty, it places greater emphasis on the ill effects of capitalism than on the ill effects of an unfettered or corrupt state. Why is this?

First, and perhaps most obvious, Pope Francis and the largely Italian Curia come from an experience of capitalism that is distorted and better characterized by crony capitalism, which indeed *has* pitted the rich and connected against the poor and nonconnected. How can one truly appreciate the benefits of capitalism when the context in which one experiences it brings out mostly the bad stuff and very little of the good?

Second, US Americans—seeped in an individualistic Protestant ethic—think very differently than Latin Americans or European Latins. Volumes have been written about these cultural differences, which clearly are broad generalizations. As they inform the pope and curia's economic views, I believe Latins have a greater comfort level with top-down, paternalistic authority and place greater emphasis on communal ties versus US Americans, who are more skeptical of centralized, overarching authority and place greater emphasis on freedom and individual achievement.

Third, I believe Pope Francis and the Roman Curia have more theoretical mind-sets than practical (i.e., business). The weakness business-minded people can fall into is thinking too narrowly and not about the broader implications of their actions. The weakness theoretical people can fall into is being blind to what works. Nothing like being responsible for a payroll to fully understand how the economy truly works, at least on the micro level.

While I would have worded a few lines about the economy differently, I fully appreciate that the pope is not writing to US Americans but rather to the world and from a distinctly Latin American perspective. The Catholic Church is concerned about the spiritual lives of people, with a special focus on the poorest and weakest among us. The church's role is not to make economic policy, and when she has crossed this line, she has gotten herself in trouble. The pope's role is not to make us feel self-pleased but to push us to grow in our faith, which often requires being challenged.

Evangelii Gaudium inspired me to start thinking more seriously about three topics I think deserve more thoughtful public discussion: (1) intrinsic differences between political power and economic wealth. Power operates on a zero-sum plane whereas wealth operates on an expansive plane. What are the implications with respect to how one views capitalism versus the state? (2) the trade-off between poverty reduction and inequality reduction? (3) different outcomes associated with addressing solidarity at the state level versus community and individual levels.

I conclude with something Father Wojciech Giertych, my professor of moral theology, explained to me this morning. Fr. Giertych is the theologian of the papal household. This post has been held by a Dominican since the Middle Ages and its job description is to provide advice to the pope on theological issues, as well as checking papal texts for theological clarity.

Fr. Giertych interprets the parable of the prodigal son as having three, not two sons. We all know about the prodigal, wastefully extravagant son and the Pharisee-like son who resents the father's mercy toward his repentant wayward son. But Fr. Giertych says there is a third son, the Father's dutiful servant who serves diligently, lovingly, and quietly in the background. The role of the pope is to help guide his flock, comprised of his two imperfect sons, to be more like his third son. *Evangelii Gaudium* has things in it that make both sons uncomfortable, which hopefully means it make them more like the third son.

CHRISTMAS DISPATCH

Christmas Eve Mass with Pope Francis

Quite an extraordinary experience last evening: up-front seats to Christmas Eve Mass with Pope Frances at St. Peter's Basilica. Normally this Mass is celebrated at midnight, but last evening they pushed it forward to 9:30 p.m. Below is a photo I snapped at the end of Mass, as Pope Frances was starting to exit.

Pope at Christmas Mass

I have Father Mark Haydu, the head of the Patrons of the Arts in the Vatican Museums Foundation, to thank for the tickets and for shepherding my parents, another American couple, and me into the Vatican at 7:30 p.m. to an up-front section reserved mostly for nuns at the side of the main altar. Father Mark knows the Vatican security protocol well and worked what seemed to me miracles to get us past the many Swiss Guards and security. He led us to four seats in the third row. The front row of our section was reserved for last-minute dignitaries, such as the king and queen of Spain, who sat there last year.

When we sat down, the basilica was dimly lit. Then the music began to play leading up to the proclamation of the birth of Christ. All of a sudden the lights were lit, creating a powerful audio and visual effect. The Mass liturgy and Pope Francis's vestments were fairly simple as far as St. Peter's fare goes. Below is the English translation of the pope's homily, which he delivered in Italian. Pope Francis seemed tired to me, which one can well understand. I couldn't help thinking how relieved Pope Emeritus Benedict, whom Pope Francis paid a special visit to a couple days ago, must have felt not having to publicly celebrate the Christmas Masses this year.

Pope Francis Christmas 2013 Homily

1. "The people who walked in darkness have seen a great light" (Isa. 9:1).

This prophecy of Isaiah never ceases to touch us, especially when we hear it proclaimed in the liturgy of Christmas night. This is not simply an emotional or sentimental matter. It moves us because it states the deep reality of what we are: a people who walk, and all around us—and within us as well—there is darkness and light. In this night, as the spirit of darkness enfolds the world, there takes place anew the event that always amazes and surprises us: the people who walk see a great light. A light that makes us reflect on this mystery: the mystery of walking and seeing.

Walking. This verb makes us reflect on the course of history, that long journey that is the history of salvation, starting with Abraham, our father in faith, whom the Lord called one day to set out, to go forth from his country toward the land that he would show him. From that time on, our identity as believers has been that of a people making its pilgrim way toward the promised land. This history has always been accompanied by the Lord! He is ever faithful to his covenant and to his promises. Because he is faithful, "God is light, and in him there is no darkness at all" (1 John 1:5). Yet on the part of the people, there are times of both light and darkness, fidelity and infidelity, obedience, and rebellion; times of being a pilgrim people and times of being a people adrift.

In our personal history too, there are both bright and dark moments, lights and shadows. If we love God and our brothers and sisters, we walk in the light; but if our hearts are closed, if we are dominated by pride, deceit, self-seeking, then darkness falls within us and around us. "Whoever hates his brother—writes the Apostle John—is in the darkness; he walks in the darkness, and does not know the way to go, because the darkness has blinded his eyes" (1 John 2:11). We are a people who walk but as a pilgrim people who do not want to go astray.

2. On this night, like a burst of brilliant light, there rings out the proclamation of the apostle: "God's grace has been revealed, and it has made salvation possible for the whole human race" (Titus 2:11).

The grace that was revealed in our world is Jesus, born of the Virgin Mary, true man and true God. He has entered our history; he has shared our journey. He came to free us from darkness and to grant us light. In him was revealed the grace, the mercy, and the tender love of the Father: Jesus is love incarnate. He is not simply a teacher of wisdom. He is not an ideal for which we strive while knowing we are hopelessly distant from it. He is the meaning of life and history, who has pitched his tent in our midst.

3. The shepherds were the first to see this "tent," to receive the news of Jesus' birth. They were the first because they were among the last, the outcast. And they were the first because they were awake, keeping watch in the night, guarding their flocks. The pilgrim is bound by duty to keep watch, and the shepherds did just that. Together with them, let us pause before the Child; let us pause in silence. Together with them, let us thank the Lord for having given Jesus to us, and with them let us raise from the depths of our hearts the praises of his fidelity. We bless you, Lord God most high, who lowered yourself for our sake. You are immense, and you made yourself small; you are rich, and you made yourself poor; you are all-powerful, and you made yourself vulnerable.

On this night let us share the joy of the gospel: God loves us. He so loves us that he gave us his Son to be our brother, to be light in our darkness. To us the Lord repeats: "Do not be afraid!" (Luke 2:10). As the angels said to the shepherds, "Do not be afraid!" And I also repeat to all of you: do not be afraid! Our Father is patient. He loves us, and he gives us Jesus to guide us on the way that leads to the Promised Land. Jesus is the light who brightens the darkness. He is mercy. Our Father always forgives us. He is our peace. Amen.

Roman Catholicism has a very earthy element to it, which was conveyed powerfully when the pope lovingly carried a figurine of Baby Jesus to a simple straw-lined cradle in front of the altar at the start of Mass and then to the large Christmas crèche after the Mass. The theology of the incarnation was represented beautifully in this simple act.

Upon exiting St. Peter's at about 11:00 p.m., we saw a sea of people in the main square, as the Mass was telecast onto the square from two large screens. There is another beautiful, life-sized Christmas crèche in the middle of the square that many people gathered around. Thankfully, it was a lovely evening, as the taxi line was very, very long, with few taxis in sight, so we walked to the metro, which ended up being closed, and there were no public buses running. So we walked and walked to Piazza Popolo (other side of the Tiber), where we were able to find a taxi to go the rest of the way to my parents' hotel.

I said a special prayer for you all on this list at Christmas Mass last evening. I wish you a happy New Year.

Ciao di Roma

DISPATCH 14

Life returned to "normal" this weekend after two weeks of visits from friends and family and an incredible Roman lead up to *Natale*. I hope all reading this are faring well, despite the crazy weather I read about on the East Coast and Midwest. It seems to me that this was a particularly good US winter to miss, and in an effort to be kind, I will not describe the [positive adjective] weather here.

Epiphany, the Real End of the Christmas Season

Tomorrow marks the end of the Christmas season in Italy, the Feast of the Epiphany, also known as the visit of the three kings or magi. Whereas in the United States, celebrations of major holy days that fall near but not on Sunday sometimes are moved to Sunday, in Italy they hold firm to the actual date. The Feast of the Epiphany is a more appreciated and celebrated feast day in Italy, as it is in Latin America. Until recently, most Latin American and Italian children received their Christmas gifts on Epiphany rather than Christmas Eve or Christmas Day. It seems to me that Americans take down their Christmas trees earlier and earlier. Last year in Maine, where I normally celebrate Christmas, I saw a number of trees being hauled to the dump on December 26. Not so in Rome, where Christmas decorations are left up until at least after Epiphany.

I took the opportunity today to read some of Pope Benedict Emeritus's Epiphany homilies and think they are among his best. One that I particularly appreciated is his January 6, 2013, homily, one of Benedict's last before his February 11, 2013, abdication announcement.

My New Favorite City in the World, Naples!

One of the major highlights of my parents' visit this Christmas was our visit to Naples, just over one hour from Rome via speed train. My very first impression, arriving in pouring rain with no one on the gritty streets, was not 100 percent positive. Due to the rain, we went straight to the Museo Archeologico Nazionale di Napoli, which houses a fantastic collection of Greek and Roman sculptures, as well as spectacular Pompeii mosaics. In the middle of an empty major ballroom-type space on the second floor is displayed the famous second-century *Farnese Atlas* sculpture, which surprised us, as it seems to reflect an understanding that that world is round by a second-century sculptor.

The museum, like the city itself, screams past glory. It was frayed, poorly organized, and poorly signed, with few security guards watching over one of the most important ancient sculpture collections in the world, and I could go on. For those who do not know Neapolitan history, Naples used to be one of the most important cities in the world strategically, politically, and artistically, saying nothing of its immense wealth. Its history, culture, and local dialect are strongly impacted by Greek, Spanish, and French influences.

I won't begin to try to explain why Naples fell off its pedestal, but it seems that Garibaldi and Italian unification in 1860–1870 (there is a lack of consensus on the actual date) is treated by Neapolitans akin to how the Civil War is viewed by many US Southerners today. At moments I felt I could be in Salvador, Bahia, Buenos Aires, or in the extreme, Havana, Cuba—once fantastically beautiful, alluring cities now ravished by age, neglect, and poverty. My first impression of Naples was definitely "third world."

But then, during the next day, touring Naples in the sun, with crowds of Neapolitans on the streets and while visiting upscale sections of the city overlooking the spectacular Bay of Naples, I was reminded of the French and Italian Riviera and could see that not all of its past glory was lost. In terms of topography, there is a great similarity between Naples and Rio de Janeiro. By day two, I was smitten—so much so that I plan to return and perhaps more than once!

Naples is fascinating, multilayered, earthy, gritty, and beautiful, not in an obvious way, in a *jolie laide* way, but in an in-your-face-yet-hidden all at the same time way. It struck me as the anti-Gnostic city *par excellence*. It is no accident that crèches (nativity scenes or *presepe* in Italian), first created by Saint Francis of Assisi, were popularized in Naples, starting in the sixteenth century. Eighteenth-century Bourbon Spanish King Charles III, ruling Naples at the time, had a special fondness for elaborate nativity scenes, which inspired even more popularity in Naples. In virtually every church we visited, prominently displayed was an elaborate *presepe*.

Caravaggio and Discovering the Museo di Capodimonte

During our second day in Naples, we visited what some consider the single most important works of art in Naples—Caravaggio's *Seven Works of Mercy*. This beautiful, complex, and difficult-to-understand painting is located in a nondescript church-museum in the heart of Naples' Centro Historico. We spent some time sitting on the wooden seats set up in front of the painting on one of the altars of a small hexagonal church to take it in.

Next we went to one of the most impressive museums I have visited, in league with El Prado and just a step below the Louvre, the Met, or the National Gallery. The Museo di Capodimonte is home to works by Botticelli, Maraccio, Titian, Correggio, Parmigianino, Lotto, Colontonio, Maraccio, Simone Martini, El Greco, Caravaggio, and Breugel. The collection of religious-inspired paintings fills floors of the museum and requires days to fully appreciate. What most impressed me was the extraordinarily high quality of the Italian painters, many Neapolitan, who are relatively unknown. Perhaps due to too-high expectations, Caravaggio's *Flagellation of Christ,* displayed prominently at the Capodimonte, proved to be one of my least-favorite Caravaggio paintings viewed in person.

The Importance of Pizza and Family

Naples guidebooks place a lot of emphasis on pizza, which was "invented" in Naples, and sure enough, I observed that pizza is indeed an integral part of this city. My parents and I ate our first (fantastic) pizza at a restaurant near the archeological museum that was relatively quiet on this rainy holiday evening. The next day, virtually every pizza place we walked by was packed with Neapolitans trying to get in or place an order.

Our second pizza of our trip was particularly special because we ate it at casa Zurlo, the home of second and third cousins, descendent from my great-grandfather. One of our Zurlo relatives, an internist doctor, insisted with all the passion a Neapolitan can muster that the family ate pizza daily because it was the "perfect" food, containing all four food groups.

Dinner culminated in dance and karaoke-like renditions (with electric piano and words on the video screen) of "O Sole Mio," "Volare," and a third Neapolitan song that I just cannot remember. It became obvious seeing the Naples Zurlos that we are blessed with a no-gray-hair gene. My father's two second cousins, who sat on the couch next to my mom, are each close to ninety years old, with practically no grey hair. It seems that love of dogs also runs in the family!

Ending the Year with Spumante and a Bang

A dear college friend and her family, including one of my godchildren, visited for New Year's, after having spent Christmas week in Cortina on a ski vacation. Unfortunately for them, it snowed so much that this upscale Italian ski resort shut down for a few days, as it could not handle all the snow.

Rome did not disappoint, though. We had a wonderful time

walking the streets and enjoying fine meals together. Splurging on an upscale restaurant, Pesa Antica, for our New Year's meal provided an important learning experience. Upon ordering prosecco to start off the evening, we were summarily informed, in a certain tone of voice, that the restaurant only served spumante, not prosecco. Renditions of cheesy Martini and Rossi Asti Spumante commercials immediately came to mind. In contrast to our American notion of prosecco being sophisticated and spumante being cheap, sweet bubbly wine, Italians consider prosceco to be the cheap cousin of spumante.

An unexpected highlight of their visit was watching New Year's fireworks from my rooftop deck. *Crazy!* The fireworks started well before midnight and went on for nearly an hour and from all angles. We stood in the middle of a 360-degree viewing of random, and what seemed to be nonofficial, firework displays shot off from all parts of Rome! It was a fantastic start of what I hope will be a joyful, peaceful year for all of you!

Un bacio di Roma

DISPATCH 15

Two More Days in Naples

My Roman sojourn comes to its end in two weeks. I am at the same time excited to come home and see my friends and family and sad to leave a place and an experience that has been fantastic. Inevitably, life has become more routine here, less intense on the senses, so when I find myself getting too comfortable, I hop on Italy's efficient, timely speed trains for a day trip or in the case of this past weekend, a Naples overnighter. I could not get enough of Naples during my family visit right after Christmas, so I returned. I spent most of my two days walking the streets of this intensely entertaining, unpredictable, beautiful, scruffy city. I plan to return yet again Saturday with visiting friends from Maine.

The spectacular view from Naples's highest point, Castel Sant'Elmo, made me fully appreciate the famous expression "*Vide Napoli e Mori*" ("See Naples, then die"). No one is certain the origin of this expression, but two theories I like attribute it to Virgil some two thousand years ago and to Goethe in the late 1780s. The castle is best reached by one of three well-functioning funiculars operating in Naples. Going by taxi takes much longer, as the roads up the hills meander back and forth in switchback fashion, and traffic can be a problem. Once I arrived at the end of the funicular line, the signage to the castle was excellent but neglected to indicate that it was still a twenty-minute or so upward climb.

The Extraordinary Cristo Velato

Michelangelo's *Pieta* has its equal in Naples. In the center of the Museo Capella Sansevero lays the *Cristo Velato* (Christ Veiled) statue by Giuseppe Sanmartino (1753). I won't even try to describe it beyond using the word *spectacular.* Surrounding this stunning masterpiece are a number of statues and an extraordinary altar relief of the Deposition. In this small, beautifully designed chapel sits a perfectly organized group of sculptures that truly takes one's breath away.

The chapel was designed by Raimondo de Sangro (1710–1771), a fascinating character described as a "nobleman, inventor, soldier, writer and scientist." Curiosity, brilliance, money, and prestige supported his pursuit of an array of personal interests, including alchemy, mechanics, sciences, and the arts. De Sangro was educated by Jesuits and came from a noble family that boasted a cardinal and a saint. His father led a wild life following the death of de Sangro's mother when de Sangro was only a few months old. As a result, de Sangro was raised by his grandfather. Like Franz Liszt, de Sangro's father, Antonio, returned to the Catholic faith of his youth, spending his final years living a very devout religious life following years of dissolute living.

After the *Veiled Christ,* the statue that de Sangro dedicated to his father, *Disillusion,* was my favorite, a man trapped in life-like ropes being freed by a winged spirit. Despite his rich Catholic heritage and education, de Sangro served as the grand master of the Masonic temple in Naples and was excommunicated by one pope, which vexed him greatly, and then un-excommunicated by a later pope. He was a complex figure to say the least.

Pizza Taken Seriously

Pizza truly is better in Naples. *Da Michele* is better known thanks to *Eat, Pray, Love* fame, but the famed *Pizzeria Sorbillo* is where I ended up, and for four Euros, I ate one of the best pizzas of my entire life.

I learned from the Cellar Tours website that there are strict rules governing Neapolitan pizza:

- It can only be cooked in wood-burning brick ovens.

- The crust has to be soft and light. That's why the dough is made the day before it's used, allowing the yeast to rise for at least ten to fifteen hours.
- The *pizzaiolo* (pizza maker) must be a real maestro: the dough-stretching technique is essential, and you need at least two to three years of apprenticeship to become a *pizzaiolo*.
- The pizzerias that make the traditional pizza *"verace"* are members of the Pizza Napoletana Association, which offers a sixty-hour "training course based on the practice and on the skills development for the manipulation of the pizza. For this reason after the theoretical lectures we organize group and individual practical work. The program is intended to give the essential concepts to understand the qualified artisanal work and to learn the Neapolitan technique."

I love how seven of the sixty hours are devoted to "theory."

A Day in Florence

Restless early one morning, I decided to spend the day in Florence, a city I hadn't been to in nearly twenty years. With Rome and Naples as my reference, it seemed much more pristine and formal to me than I had remembered. Florence is a city of superlatives, and it is nearly impossible to write anything original about this extraordinary jewel. Something that was different from my last visit was the fact that practically every church I entered required paid admission. Churches have become museums rather than sacred spaces. I fully understand why it has come to this, but it saddened me.

A highlight of my day was a visit to Biblioteca Medicea Laurenziana Firenze (Laurentian Library), the repository of thousands of manuscripts and early printed books. Michelangelo designed the library, and the entryway staircase (a ubiquitous Art

History 101 slide) is stunningly beautiful. Also stunning are the unique stained glass windows with white backgrounds and beautiful, intricate designs of plants, animals, coats of arms, etc. I had never seen anything like them.

On display was an exhibit of Boccaccio's handwritten books and manuscripts, which I found fascinating for the single reason that they are the only ancient (fourteenth century if that counts as ancient) books I have seen with words and phrases actually crossed out and rewritten. I had wondered how one could write original pieces or even transcribe works and make no mistakes. Mistakes were made!

Boccaccio, who was born in Florence but lived a large chunk of his young adult life in Naples, was a confrere of Dante. Both wrote in the Italian vernacular, revolutionary at the time. Boccaccio is known for his juicy, realistic dialogue and unforgiving and astute character portrayals. Some believe that Chaucer's *Canterbury Tales*, also written in the vernacular, were influenced by Boccoccio's *Decameron*.

My Florence indulgence was the purchase of a handmade pair of gorgeous Quercioli shoes. I came to Rome with a suitcase full of books, and I will be returning to New York City with a suitcase full of shoes.

I finish this dispatch with a fantastic quote. Before coming to Rome, a friend of mine gave me the book, *Italian Ways: On and Off the Trains from Milan to Palermo*, by British author Tim Parks, who has lived in Italy for decades. His summation of Italians, as an Anglo-Saxon observer: "In every aspect of Italian life, one of the key characteristics to get to grips with is that this is a nation at ease with the distance between ideal and real. They are beyond what we call hypocrisy. Quite simply they do not register the contradiction between rhetoric and behavior. It is an enviable mind-set."

Un bacio di Roma

DISPATCH 16

Studying at the University of an Angel

My Roman sojourn has been extraordinarily special, largely because of two classes I audited at the Angelicum, formally named the Pontificia Universita S. Tommaso D'Aquino. I do not exaggerate when I say that my normally restless mind did not wander for a single moment during the four hours of class lectures I attended each week.

The Angelicum

What is a pontifical university? According to the Holy See (Vatican), pontifical universities are "academic institutes established or approved directly by the Holy See, composed of three main ecclesiastical faculties (Theology, Philosophy and Canon Law) and at least one other faculty. These academic institutes deal specifically with the Christian revelation and related disciplines, and the Church's mission of spreading the Gospel ..." Technically, pontifical universities report to Rome, but, *de facto*, they are fairly independent, like so many elements of the Catholic Church, belying the widely held notion that Rome micromanages the entire Catholic Church. This is a major topic of theological and political debate/discussion from which I flee.

Like European and US universities, pontifical universities offer three levels of degrees corresponding to a bachelor's, master's, and doctorate, and most Catholic bishops (and therefore, cardinals) have at least the equivalent of a master's, if not a doctorate, in sacred theology (STD). Incidentally, during the election of Pope Francis, some commentaries highlighted the small number of Latin American cardinals relative to the number of Latin American Roman Catholics. An important reason: fewer Latin American priests have advanced degrees. There are some sixty-five pontifical universities throughout the world, nineteen in Latin America and seven in the United States, the main one being Catholic University in DC, where I soon will be teaching full-time.

The Angelicum is one of eleven pontifical universities located in Rome itself. Each pontifical university is run by a different religious order of the Catholic Church, though there may be some nuanced exceptions that I do not know about. Accordingly, each has a very distinct personality and theological emphasis.

The Angelicum was established in 1222 by the Dominican order, whose most prominent member was Thomas Aquinas (d. 1274), arguably *the* most brilliant mind of the Catholic Church of all ages. I felt especially inspired to send this dispatch today, as today is the feast day of St. Thomas Aquinas, referred to as the angelic doctor of the church because, according to Pope Benedict XVI, the title expresses "the sublimity of his thought and the purity of his life." Now you know why the university is nicknamed the Angelicum.

Thomas Aquinas's seminal work, *Summa Theologica,* is the classic text for Catholic education, of which Aquinas is the patron saint. In addition to being brilliant, Aquinas was also a very holy man. Three months before Aquinas died, while celebrating Mass, he received a revelation that so affected him that he never wrote another word afterward. In response to his secretary's pleas to finish his work, Aquinas replied, "The end of my labors has come. All that I have written appears to be as so much straw after the things that have been revealed to me ... I can write no more. I have seen things that make my writings like straw."

Grace versus Nature

There is friendly rivalry between the Roman pontifical universities, mirroring the (mostly) good natured rivalry between religious orders. One of the longest standing "rivalries" between religious orders is that between Dominicans and Jesuits. I mention this because I am fascinated by the grace-nature relationship, a difficult but immensely important issue that has challenged theologians and lay people since the beginning of Christianity. Understanding the nature-grace trade-off is also relevant to an understanding of God's covenant with Israel, so Jewish Talmud scholars also grapple with this issue. Excommunications have been handed down and wars fought over where the *pura natura* line ends and God's *gratia* begins.

Historically, the Jesuits and Dominicans have held different views on the relative dynamics and workings of grace and nature. Generalizing, I think it is fair to say that the Jesuits, rooted in the views of the somewhat controversial sixteenth-century theologian Luis Molina, place a greater emphasis on the importance of human will, as it relates to grace's workings, than the Dominican Thomists, who emphasize a greater distinction between human nature (or will) and grace, ceding a bit more power to grace. Jesuits have been known to accuse Dominican Thomists of being dualists, and Dominicans (and others) have been known to accuse Jesuits of being semi-Pelagianists. Ouch!

Good-Natured Rivalries

Returning to more earthly matters, what is very clear to the eye is that the various Roman pontifical universities vary greatly in their funding and hence, physical plants. The two spiffiest pontifical universities I saw were the Jesuit Gregorian and the Opus Dei Santa Croce. The Angelicum is among the lowliest when it comes to physical plant but I nonobjectively argue, the best when it comes to solid theology, especially Thomist theology.

I chuckled when an Opus Dei priest I met quipped, in response to my amazement at the Santa Croce facilities relative to the Angelicum facilities, that "poor doesn't equate to shabbiness." The reaction of a Jesuit friend while visiting the Angelicum with me was, "I need to work hard fundraising to make sure the Gregorian keeps its lead."

One of my Dominican professors explained to me that the reason the Angelicum physical plant is in a state of benign neglect is because the Dominicans are a decentralized order and don't pay as much attention to their one centralized institution, the Angelicum. In contrast, the Jesuits are a "military" order, managed from the top down, with the Gregorian enjoying a special place of pride and hence, greater resources and attention.

My favorite "rivalry" comment came from my other Dominican professor who smilingly asserted, "Since Pope Francis canonized one of Ignatius Loyola's confreres, Peter Faber, last week [without a miracle under a papal bull thing called 'equivalent canonization'], I would next expect him to canonize [sixteenth-century Dominican defender of Latin American indigenous] Bartolome de las Casas!" This friendly, goodhearted rivalry reflects a bit of humanity that I love, though, sadly, religious rivalries have also devolved into some pretty ugly stuff in the past and well into the present.

What nearly every non-American priest I met spoke enviously

about was the residence where American seminarians and priests live while studying in Rome, nicknamed the NAC (North American College). It is located on Juniculum Hill with fantastic views of Rome and more important, fantastic sports facilities, including a top-notch soccer field. This provides the North American seminarians with an "unfair" advantage in the annual Clericus Cup soccer tournament comprised of teams from the various seminaries in Rome, largely delineated by geography. The North Americans are the current champions.

Thomas Aquinas and the Mystics

The two classes I audited were "Christian Faith, Hope, and Charity"—"The theological virtues through which a contact with God is established and developed are studied according to their presentation in the Summa of Theology of Aquinas"—taught by the brilliant Papal Theologian, Fr. Wojciech Giertych, and "Spiritual Theology"—"The invitation to spiritual communion with God as presented in the First Letter of St. John. Study of selected texts from the Christian spiritual tradition (e.g., Ignatius of Antioch, Letter to the Romans, St. Augustine, Confessions) with special emphasis on the following themes: God's saving mercy, prayer, the ascetical life, growth in holiness and contemporary spirituality"—taught by Fr. Paul Murray.

I chose these two courses solely because of the professors. I had the privilege of hearing both speak in the United States before coming to Rome, so I knew ahead of time that they were fantastic lecturers, in addition to being highly renowned. Fr. Giertych is a Thomist through and through, which means his approach and delivery is incredibly logical and systematic. I considered this my "physics" class, filled mostly with guys, priests in this case, as I was one of the few lay people in the class.

Thomas Aquinas's writings are a monumental cornerstone of Catholic theology and are absolutely critical to understand if one wants to deeply understand Christian theology. However, he is not that easy to read, even after being translated from the Latin, certainly not someone you would read during a leisurely Saturday night. Fr. Giertych can be a bit intimidating, but underneath his stern, Polish demeanor is a deeply holy teddy bear of a man with a sharp, dry sense of humor. I cannot thank him enough for acquainting me with one of the world's most profound thinkers, Thomas Aquinas.

Fr. Giertych's apartment is very close to the papal apartment, which is now empty owing to Pope Francis's decision to live in a nearby residence instead. Visiting Fr. Giertych gives one a full appreciation of why Pope Francis made this decision: Living in the apostolic palace truly is living in a museum-like prison, with long, dark corridors, decorated with Michelangelo and Rafael frescos, protected by many layers of Swiss guard security. On the walls of a long hallway inside Fr. Giertych's apartment are paintings of all the papal theologians going back many centuries, all of whom are Dominican.

In contrast, Fr. Murray is a poet, with a mellifluous, Irish-accented voice. Though Dominican, he has a profound understanding and sensitivity to Carmelite spirituality. We spent a fair amount of time on St. Teresa of Avila, St. John of the Cross, St. Therese de Lisieux—three major contemplative saints and all doctors of the Catholic Church—St. Augustine, Catherine of Siena, and Bernard de Clairvaux. Fr. Murray's class was a bit more accessible, though no less profound, and had many more lay people and nuns. He has written many books on prayer and contemplation, in addition to books of poetry.

The saint Fr. Murray spent the most time on was St. Augustine. For anyone who has not yet read St. Augustine's *Confessions*, I say run out now and get the book. Though Augustine lived in the fifth century, his self-reflections are extraordinarily relevant today. He was the naval gazer *par excellence,* and one of the many lines of his that I love is, "Who am I? I am an enigma to myself. You, alone, Lord, know who I am." St. Augustine spent his early life obsessively searching for the truth, and once he found truth, he obsessively worked on understanding himself in relationship to God. Parts of the *Confessions* read almost like a Woody Allen dialogue.

On this high note, I end my dispatches from Rome. I return to crazy cold NYC this Friday, excited to come home and see friends and family but also naturally saddened that something so wonderful is coming to an end. I can't begin to voice my appreciation for this opportunity, which has given me much-needed rest from many, many years of tireless work and travel, an opportunity to experience intense beauty, learn more about the profoundly rich Catholic faith, meet extraordinary people, create a collection of memories that will last a lifetime, and enjoy the best food and wine in the world!

Ciao di Roma

POST SCRIPTUM

The last thirty hours of my Roman sabbatical were among the most memorable, so I am writing a last dispatch. On Thursday morning, Fr. Mark Haydu, the priest who runs the Patrons of the Arts of the Vatican Museums Foundation, the same priest who arranged for our Christmas Eve Mass, celebrated a private Mass for me at the tomb of St. Peter, located directly beneath the main altar of St. Peter's Basilica. Below is a photo Fr. Peter kneeling at the altar, and one can see the windowed pane, behind which are St. Peter's bones. It was one of the most memorable Masses I ever experienced and one of the top highlights of my Roman stay.

Father Mark at the tomb of St. Peter

I met Fr. Mark a few minutes before seven in the morning at a side gate leading to the area behind St. Peter's Basilica. We entered the basilica through a private entrance, along with nearly two dozen other priests also there to celebrate private Masses in the various tombs of the crypt of St. Peter's, where many popes are buried. The priests moved hastily. I later learned it was "first come, first serve" in terms of which papal tomb a priest was given permission to celebrate Mass. Fr. Mark quickly ushered me into a very large sacristy, where the priests put on their Mass vestments and collect the sacred vessels used to celebrate Mass.

I had never been in a sacristy while a priest was preparing for Mass. To see dozens of priests in this setting expertly and rapidly getting ready was extraordinary. I was touched that the only painting in the sacristy was one depicting Father Vianney (Cure d'Ars), a very holy, very simple eighteenth-century French country priest who is the patron saint of priests. Father Vianney did so poorly in his studies, especially Latin, that he nearly was prevented from priestly ordination. This is the saint whose image is prominently displayed in one of the most exalted places on earth and among the church's most-learned and sophisticated priests about to celebrate Mass. What a beautiful message of humility.

That night I was awakened by a powerful thunderstorm and heavy rain. It rained a fair amount during my stay in Rome, so I did not think much about it until my landlord, who came to bid me good-bye Friday morning, could not reach any taxi company by phone to order me a taxi to the airport. It reminded me of NYC rush hour in the rain, when finding taxis is nearly impossible. After many tries to established taxi companies, he remembered someone in the Trastevere neighborhood who once drove him somewhere years ago named Rocco. My landlord rang Rocco, woke him up, and pleaded with him to take me to the airport.

After a thirty-minute wait in the doorway of my apartment building, under pouring rain, Rocco drove up to the rescue. Rather calmly, he informed me that Rome was flooded, the highway to the airport was closed, and the train tracks between the city center and the airport were flooded but not to worry because he knew back roads to the airport. Nearly two hours later, we finally arrived, after being turned back at many junctures by police blocking flooded roads. We saw walls crumbled into streets, overflowing rivers, and fields that had become mini lakes. I arrived with not a minute to spare, one of the last to board a partially empty plane right before takeoff, as many others never made it. I truly believe Rocco (rock, *Cephas*, Peter) was a miracle sent by St. Peter himself.

With thanks to St. Peter, I say a final *arrivederci* to Rome (for now),

Luanne

CPSIA information can be obtained at www.ICGtesting.com
Printed in the USA
BVOW02s1509171114

375459BV00001B/2/P